Virtue Hoarders

Forerunners: Ideas First

Short books of thought-in-process scholarship, where intense analysis, questioning, and speculation take the lead

FROM THE UNIVERSITY OF MINNESOTA PRESS

(Continued on page 81)

Virtue Hoarders
The Case against the Professional
Managerial Class

Catherine Liu

University of Minnesota Press
MINNEAPOLIS
LONDON

ISBN 978-1-5179-1225-3 (PB)
ISBN 978-1-4529-6604-5 (Ebook)
ISBN 978-1-4529-6644-1 (Manifold)

Published by the University of Minnesota Press
111 Third Avenue South, Suite 290
Minneapolis, MN 55401–2520
http://www.upress.umn.edu

Available as a Manifold edition at manifold.umn.edu

The University of Minnesota is an equal-opportunity educator and employer.

Contents

Contents

Introduction

FOR AS LONG as most of us can remember, the professional managerial class (PMC) has been fighting a class war, not against capitalists or capitalism, but against the working classes. Members of the PMC have memories of a time when they were more progressive—during the Progressive Era, specifically. They once supported working-class militancy in its epic struggles against robber barons and capitalists like Mrs. Leland Stanford Jr., Andrew Carnegie, John D. Rockefeller, and Andrew Mellon, but today, they go to Stanford and view private foundations bearing those same names as models of philanthropy and sources of critical funding and recognition. They still believe themselves to be the heroes of history, fighting to defend innocent victims against their evil victimizers, but the working class is not a group they find worth saving, because by PMC standards, they do not behave properly: they are either disengaged politically or too angry to be civil. Liberal members of the credentialed classes love to use the word *empower* when they talk about "people," but the use of that verb objectifies the recipients of their help while implying that the people have no access to power without them. The PMC as a proxy for today's ruling class is shameless about hoarding all forms of secularized virtue: whenever it addresses a political and economic crisis produced by capitalism itself, the PMC reworks political struggles for policy change and redistribution into individual passion plays, focusing its efforts on individual acts of "giving back" or reified forms of self-transformation. It finds in its particular tastes and cultural proclivities the justification for its unshakable sense of superiority to ordinary working-class people. If its politics amount to little more than virtue signaling, it loves nothing more than moral panics to incite its members to ever more pointless forms of pseudo-politics and hypervigilance. The much-maligned Hillary Clinton was honest in her contempt for ordinary people when, in 2016, she dismissed Trump supporters as "deplorables." Their 2016 defiance of PMC and liberal nostra has only hardened into reactionary antiauthoritarianism, which another reactionary demagogue will seek to exploit. PMC virtue hoarding is the insult added to injury when white-collar managers, having downsized their blue-collar workforce, then disparage them for their bad taste in literature, bad diets, unstable families, and deplorable child-rearing habits.

When the PMC sympathized with the plight of masses of working people, it also pioneered professional standards of research grounded in professional organizations like the American Medical Association, the Association of University Professors, and all the professional organizations that currently dominate academic life. In organizing professional life, the PMC tried to protect the integrity of specialists and experts against the power of capitalists and the markets. From Jane Addams to John Dewey, members of the early American PMC established academic freedom and the role of research in guiding public policy as critical to the development of industrial democracy. In doing so, the first social workers, muckraking journalists and radical social scientists, were following the lead of American workers and the Socialist Party led by Eugene Debs in a millennial struggle for worker power.[1] Those heady days of PMC heroism are long gone. The PMC, with its professional discipline and aura of disinterestedness, did very well for itself during the Depression, during World War II, and in the postwar period with the expansion of universities and the growing complexity of the American and social economic order. When the tide turned against American workers, the PMC preferred to fight culture wars against the classes below while currying the favor of capitalists it once despised. The culture war was always a proxy economic war, but the 1960s divided the country into the allegedly enlightened and the allegedly benighted, with the PMC able to separate itself from its economic inferiors in a way that seemed morally justifiable.

It was after 1968 that the PMC gradually shifted its allegiance from workers to capital. Since that time, the most successful and visible segments of the PMC have brazenly put their smarts at the service of the bosses. If Marx theorized that class struggle was the engine of historical change and the political agent of it the proletariat, the newest incarnation of the PMC tries to make history by undermining working-class power and ignoring working-class interests. The post-1968 PMC elite has become ideologically convinced of its own unassailable position as comprising the most advanced people the earth has ever seen. They have, in fact, made a virtue of their vanguardism. Drawing on the legacy of the counterculture and its commitment to technological and spiritual innovations, PMC elites try to tell the rest of us how to live, and in large part, they have succeeded in destroying and building in its own image the physical and now cybernetic

1. Steve Fraser, *The Age of Acquiescence: The Life and Death of American Resistance to Organized Wealth and Power* (New York: Basic Books, 2015).

infrastructure of our everyday lives.[2] As the fortunes of the PMC elites rose, the class insisted on its ability to do ordinary things in extraordinary, fundamentally superior and more virtuous ways: as a class, it was reading books, raising children, eating food, staying healthy, and having sex as the most culturally and affectively advanced people in human history. While the conservative critique of this "new" class, whether from Herman Kahn, William F. Buckley, Newt Gingrich, or David Brooks and Tucker Carlson, is pure media theater, its condemnation of liberalism's secret contempt for ordinary people rings true. Right-wing pundits heard the rage of ordinary people, but they weaponized that feeling for reactionary political purposes. No one has been as effective at mobilizing popular resentment of the PMC as Donald Trump. He merely stepped in to take advantage of decades of successful conservative propaganda positioning PMC liberalism as the enemy of the people and popular interests. Trump never pretended to be virtuous: his id-driven politics and lack of self-control formed the core of his appeal to those who felt scorned by the liberal superego. To defeat reactionary politics masquerading as populism, we need anti-PMC class struggle from the Left, not more identity politics, which has become just another vehicle of PMC virtue signaling. The Democratic Party, however, is not the political organization that will lead us in a struggle against capitalism and its deeply destructive system of exploitation and rent seeking.

My brief introduction to the PMC is polemical: for a recent "objective" account of the term, one need look no further than Gabriel Winant's "Professional Managerial Chasm: a Sociological

2. Michael Pollan's account in *The Omnivore's Dilemma: A Natural History of Four Meals* (New York: Penguin 2006) of People's Park, food co-ops, and the organic food industry tells a fascinating part of the story of countercultural aspirations.

Designation Turned into an Epithet and Hurled Like a Missile," for *N+1*.[3] Unlike Winant's article, the work represented here is not a neutral piece of professional scholarship, refining terms and their definitions, insisting on nuance, and then finger wagging at those on the Left who are allegedly uncivil, who cannot hold polite discussions, and who hurl epithets at their enemies like missiles. Winant believes in liberal virtue; I do not. Winant published his PMC apologia and his left-bashing article at a time when Elizabeth Warren was leading in the 2019 polls, before voting began in the Democratic primaries. Warren failed to place second or sometimes even third or fourth in all the states that voted. Winant urged Sanders's supporters to bend the knee and reconcile themselves to Warren's brand of progressive professionalism. He did not foresee that it was Sanders who would win primary after primary while voters resoundingly rejected Warren's brand of limited progressivism.

The reasons for this rejection are manifold, but centrists and liberals want to ignore popular distrust of incremental solutionism by dismissing the collective desire for radical economic reorganization. In the United States, generations of allegedly neutral experts have hollowed out public goods, degraded the public sphere, facilitated the monetization of everything from health to aptitude, and indebted generations of Americans in a fantasy of meritocracy enhanced social mobility.[4] Liberals have sat by while finance capital and corporate interests gutted the public treasury. Winant, however, historicizes the PMC and asks

---

3. Gabriel Winant, "Professional Managerial Chasm," *n+1*, October 19, 2019, https://nplusonemag.com/online-only/online-only/professional-managerial-chasm/.

4. For more on this topic, see Leo Krapp and Catherine Liu, "Meritocracy Agonistes," *Damage Magazine,* September 1, 2020, https://damagemag.com/2020/08/31/meritocracy-agonistes/.

us not to abandon its values. In criticizing the PMC by offering a polemical account of its morals, I hope to weaken its power over the way we think about politics. The endgame in my critique is a return to socialist politics and socialist policies, once marginalized by PMC thought leaders and made visible by the historic 2016 and 2020 presidential campaigns of Bernie Sanders. Now that we have seen the results of the 2020 Democratic primaries, however, I am even more sure that Warren and the rest of the PMC will be standing in the way of real political change. Angling for a place in the new Biden administration, Warren has proven herself more interested in her own professional ascendancy than in the political ideology and social values that she and Sanders are supposed to share.

According to John and Barbara Ehrenreich, the PMC is made up of "salaried mental workers who do not own the means of production and whose major function in the social division of labor may be described broadly as the reproduction of capitalist culture and capitalist class relations."[5] While Siegfried Kracauer and C. Wright Mills described white-collar workers as clerks, salespeople, and office workers who were shielded from physical labor, the Ehrenreichs' PMC comprises de-racinated, credentialed professionals, such as culture industry creatives, journalists, software engineers, scientists, professors, doctors, bankers, and lawyers, who play important managerial roles in large organizations. During the 1960s, young members of the class saw Robert McNamara, prosecutor of the Vietnam War, as the clear enemy of progress: for them McNamara was a cold-

---

5. John Ehrenreich and Barbara Ehrenreich, "The Professional-Managerial Class," in *Between Labor and Monopoly Capital,* ed. Pat Walker, 5–48 (Boston: South End Press, 1979), originally published as "The New Left and the Professional-Managerial Class," *Radical America* 11, no. 3 (1977).

blooded killer, but he was simply a very high level member of their class. Today's PMC may not wear pocket protectors, but it has overseen the devastation of the lives and livelihoods of poor and working-class Americans of all races, genders, and sexualities in the name of equality of opportunity, competitiveness, austerity, and efficiency. Since the 1970s, PMC elites have been happy to abandon mass politics to reproduce the social division of labor and the widening gulf between those who prosper under late capitalism and those who do not.

American conservatives have shown themselves more willing to talk about class antagonism than liberals like Winant. For instance, in an article called "The Real Class War," *American Affairs* editor Julius Krein described the current political situation in America as one shaped by class war between the 0.01 percent and the top 10 percent, or the PMC. For him, the American working class has been so beaten down that it has no political agency at all. For Krein, a better, more enlightened PMC has to emerge to reverse policies that have intensified inequality across every economic stratum. More militant than Winant, Krein urged PMC elites to act in their self-interest to fight against "intra-elite inequality: in order to help the immiserated working class to overthrow our own 'pathetic' oligarchs, the lower tiers of the PMC must lead the fight against alienation and exploitation."[6] In the same issue of *American Affairs,* Krein published Amber Frost's "The Characterless Opportunism of the Managerial Class," a counterpoint article in which the author argues that the PMC is composed of unreliable, shape-shifting "rear guarders."[7]

---

6. Julius Krein, "The Real Class War," American Affairs 3, no. 4 (2019), https://americanaffairsjournal.org/2019/11/the-real-class-war/.
7. Amber Frost, "The Characterless Opportunism of the Managerial Class," *American Affairs* 3, no. 4 (2019), https:// americanaffairsjournal.org/2019/11/the-characterless-opportunism-of -the-managerial-class/.

In 2019, Michael Lind published *The New Class War: Saving Democracy from the Managerial Elite*. In this book, Lind wants to resuscitate the American ideal of a classless society, and he blames the managerial elite for the rise of Anglo-American populism. I do not entirely disagree. Lind also denounces the PMC for its demonization of the working-class rejection of centrist incrementalism. Lind is that strangest of creatures, an antisocialist advocate for working-class power.[8] As such, he is able to address the failings of Occupy Wall Street and its neglect of class conflict for anarchist proceduralism and the cultural turn that facilitated such politics, but his goal of securing a lasting class peace implies a neat, negotiated resolution to class antagonism that is managerial and administrative rather than political and objective. What terrifies Lind and most centrists, conservative and liberal, is the idea that really, implemented socialism, as a form of political governance, is not the end of class struggle but only its real beginning.

As a class, the PMC loves to talk about bias rather than inequality, racism rather than capitalism, visibility rather than exploitation. Tolerance for them is the highest secular virtue—but tolerance has almost no political or economic meaning. The Right is well aware of liberal preening, and it has weaponized popular resentment against this class of alleged hypocrites. Fox

---

8. To strengthen the working class in its struggle for legitimacy against the domination of what Lind calls the managerial elites, he argues for the restoration of working-class power in its historic forms: against economic domination, the guild would represent working-class interests; the ward would represent working-class interests in the realms of government and culture—"the congregation would exercise countervailing power on behalf of working-class citizens against media elites and overclass academic elites." Michael Lind, *The New Class War: Saving Democracy from the Managerial Elite* (New York: Penguin Portfolio, 2020), 136.

News lives to own liberals; reactionary hatred of professionals and professionalism come not out of love for the people but out of fealty to the special sovereignty of free markets to solve all social problems. In fact, conservatives need a functioning and powerful PMC cadre of inhibited professionals to serve as punching bags for their politics of popular resentment. The PMC continues to oblige these reactionaries by betraying popular policies like Medicare for All, opting instead for means-tested, think tank–brewed Big Pharma and lobbyist-approved forms of health care that allow for profit taking to take place at the expense of public health and health care workers. Insurance companies have doubled their profits since the beginning of the coronavirus pandemic. Their most powerful lobbyists have the Democratic Party in their thrall. It turns out that PMC virtue is also the color of money.

Although the PMC is profoundly secular in nature, its rhetorical tone is pseudo-religious. While the PMC infuriates conservative Christians with its media monopoly on liberal righteousness, it finds salvation, like most Protestant sects, in material and earthly success. In liberal circles, talking about class or class consciousness before other forms of difference is not just controversial; it is heretical.[9] They call you a "class reductionist" if you argue that race, gender, and class are not interchangeable categories. They pile on with the legalistic and deadly term *intersectional* to accommodate the materialist critique of their politics. The PMC simply does not want its class identity or interests unmasked. Young people wanting to en-

9. See Adolph Reed's banning by the New York Democratic Socialists of America. Michael Powell, "A Black Marxist Scholar Wanted to Talk about Race: It Ignited a Fury," *New York Times,* August 14, 2020, https://www.nytimes.com/2020/08/14/us/adolph-reed-controversy.html.

ter what the Ehrenreichs called the "liberal professions" and gain positions in academia and the culture and media industries have had to adapt themselves to the Procrustean bed of PMC-dominated networks of influence. Anyone who wants to privilege class critique should be prepared to be thoroughly red-baited and asked questions like "Why do you wear presentable clothes when you're a socialist? Shouldn't you wear burlap sacks?" and "Why do you enjoy sports? Isn't that part of the military–industrial complex?" and "Why do you encourage conflict? Aren't you irresponsibly fomenting violence?" PMC elites believe that asceticism is the fate of the leftist and that any kind of social conflict arising from corrosive inequality is her fault. In promoting these casual assumptions about leftism, the PMC defends capitalism as the purveyor of both luxury and harmony. Gabriel Winant's characterization of the Left's warlike language is just one example of liberalism's attempts to discipline its antagonist, the socialist who takes issue with the PMC. What leftists must accept is that for us, there is no class without class antagonism and class contradiction. I do not opine on the PMC because I hope to have a civil discussion about our differences: I am writing this critique to isolate the PMC's historically grounded, virtue-hoarding politics of liberal refusal to adopt and support the social and political changes we desperately need.

In 1977, the Ehrenreichs were the first to predict that PMC values and ideology would dominate liberal and eventually neoliberal politics for the foreseeable future. Since they published their essay, the class and its defining characteristics have evolved and morphed as its powers have expanded and capitalism has become even more predatory. In fact, the fungibility of the PMC is part of the class's structural dynamism. The Ehrenreichs' analysis allows us to isolate and identify the hegemony of a class that has, in its most recent incarnation, become desperate to hold on to the power it has accrued since the 1970s.[10] The dark social consequences of its monopoly on expertise, in addition to its attempts to monopolize public virtue while blocking any attempts at meaningful economic redistribution, have given shape to our present political situation.

The Ehrenreichs drew from Siegfried Kracauer's study of interwar salaried masses in Berlin, who were the quintessentially deluded political subjects. They despised anyone who did physical labor and dreamed about instant luxury and wealth while enthusiastically writing their own pink slips. C. Wright Mills condemned the postwar white-collar worker as hopelessly identified with selling and thought of this particular worker as particularly susceptible to market discipline and its prefab, reified versions of personality and intersubjectivity. Christopher Lasch believed the white-collar, managerial classes to be hopelessly and collectively hypnotized by their own narcissism.[11] For the Ehrenreichs, the contemporary PMC embodies all of these qualities identified by left social critics of the past, but the new elites of this class have weaponized their identification with capitalism. Even though they look down on the vulgarity and stupidity of the masses, they are entirely indifferent and even hostile to the professional protocols and norms defended by their liberal precursors. They actually hold in high value a tradition- and history-busting form of entrepreneurialism that courts publicity and hates hierarchy and organization.

10. Ehrenreich and Ehrenreich, "Professional-Managerial Class."

11. Siegfried Kracauer, *The Salaried Masses: Duty and Distraction in Weimar Germany,* trans. Quentin Hoare (London: Verso, 1998); C. Wright Mills, *White Collar: The American Middle Classes* (London: Oxford University Press, 2002); Christopher Lasch, *The Culture of Narcissism: American Life in an Age of Diminishing Expectations* (New York: W. W. Norton, 2018).

Since you are reading this book, you are probably, like me, an ambivalent member of the PMC. I am at best a second-generation PMC person, but I do not like what I see of my class, and I am determined to fight to socialize the things that the PMC wants to hoard: virtue, grit, persistence, erudition, specialized knowledge, prestige, and pleasure, along with cultural and actual capital. To define the changing contours of a class to which one partially belongs is to enter into the difficult process of political self-criticism, beginning with an exfoliating and brutal reconceptualization and historicization of one's own values, sensibilities, and affects. To renounce one's narcissistic fetishization of intelligence or refinement is not a simple act. This short introduction aims at helping us do the necessary work of self-criticism while providing a few tools to attack PMC positions in its best-defended redoubts—political organizations, publishing, media, private foundations, think tanks, and the university.

While the Right represents an obdurate obstacle to economic reorganization and large-scale social redistribution, it is actually the liberal PMC that stands in the way of the political revolution necessary to forge a different kind of society and world, one in which the dignity of ordinary people and the working class takes center stage. The PMC is deeply hostile to simple redistributive policies that a Bernie Sanders presidency would have implemented: it is against the idea of building solidarity among the oppressed. It prefers obscurantism, balkanization, and management of interest groups to a transformative reimagination of the social order. It wants to play the virtuous social hero, but as a class, it is hopelessly reactionary. The interests of the PMC are now tied more than ever to its corporate overlords than to the struggles of the majority of Americans whose suffering is merely background décor for the PMC's elite volunteerism. Members of the PMC soften the sharpness of their guilt about collective suffering by stroking their credentials and telling themselves that they are better and more qualified to lead and guide than other people.

PMC centrism is a powerful ideology. Its priorities in research and innovation have been shaped more and more by corporate interests and the profit motive, while in the humanities and social sciences, scholars are rewarded by private foundations for their general disregard for historical knowledge, not to mention historical materialism. The rewards for following ruling-class directives are just too great, but the intellectual and psychic price that has to be paid for compliance should be too high for any member of society. In academia, the American PMC has achieved a great deal in establishing the rigors of peer review consensus and research autonomy, but we can no longer afford to defend its cherished principle of epistemological neutrality as a secret weapon against "extremism." We live in a political, environmental, and social emergency: class war over distribution of resources is the critical battle of our times.

In *Fear of Falling: The Inner Life of the Middle Class,* Barbara Ehrenreich's follow-up to the 1977 essay on the PMC, Ehrenreich argued that growing PMC class antagonism against working-class people was animated by growing economic fear in reaction to right-wing attacks on social and public services, now combined with countercultural contempt for ordinary people. By the Reagan era, the hippie had morphed into the yuppie, or young urban professional, who could boast of an intense attachment to the nonpareil pleasures and instant gratifications enabled by the American Express card.[12] As economic redistribution from top to bottom came to an end, and rent-seeking capitalists were

---

12. Barbara Ehrenreich, *Fear of Falling: The Inner Life of the Middle Class* (New York: Twelve, 2020).

no longer vilified in the popular imagination, the yuppie briefly took center stage in the American imagination as a figure who pointed the way to a gaudy, self-indulgent future. According to Ehrenreich, the yuppie reconciled 1960s hedonism and 1980s debt-fueled consumerism. Prayer beads became Rolexes, but the tradition-busting ethos was the same: pleasure will set you free. The young urban professional mocked the ideals of economic disinterestedness and elite public service that had characterized the old PMC. The celebration of the pure power of money was embodied both by the fictional Patrick Bateman, the homeless and prostitute-murdering, coke-addled Wall Street trader of *American Psycho,* and the real-life Donald Trump. In *American Psycho,* Bret Easton Ellis makes yuppie sadism seem *transgressively* antiliberal, exciting, and glamorous.[13]

By the 1980s, PMC elite fantasies about ordinary middle-, lower-middle-, and working-class Americans were colored by both yuppie and hippie fantasies: ordinary people were trapped in stultifying stable jobs, deferred gratification, and social conformity. They were like Flaubert's village idiots, but infuriatingly, they enjoyed good pensions and benefits. If the hippies hated the stability achieved by the union-negotiated peace with postwar corporations, yuppies actually went ahead and destroyed the institutions of lifetime-guaranteed employment through leveraged buyouts that led to blue- and then white-collar downsizing. Yuppies were not American psychos or charismatic sociopaths— they were boring, anxious, and conformist— but they did represent a new face of the PMC elite: they served new masters and enjoyed the rewards of that service. When Jack Welch took over General Electric in 1981, he personified as a super yuppie the ethos of management for stockholder value. Welch relied on a

13. Bret Easton Ellis, *American Psycho* (New York: Vintage, 1991).

cadre of PMC cost cutters and "set out to raise the stock price by cutting the workforce."[14] More than seventy thousand GE employees lost their jobs on Welch's watch, and his managerial abilities were loudly celebrated in the business press and across business schools all over the world. Stockbrokers and upper management were well rewarded for their work in downsizing workforces. Yuppies helped to birth a new world for capitalism, a world of public austerity and private luxury, globalized economies and shiny cities surrounded by devastated hinterlands, a world of offshored labor and lightning-quick capital flows. They executed neoliberalism's orders, and they snorted coke while they were at it, their alleged vanguardism only limited by their credit card limits.

The more Reagan tore away at the social safety net, the more the poor appeared to the fragile middle class as nightmarish doubles of who they would be if they were to lose their toeholds on bourgeois respectability. The PMC saw the classes below them through the eyes of the ruling class, and they could not distance themselves fast enough from the immiserated poor. As downward social mobility became a terrifying reality, poor people were increasingly seen as the monstrous other. Poverty was racialized and the poor were demonized in right-wing talking points. In the time of Reagan, a new narrative of poverty emerged: poor people had no impulse control. They did not live within their means: the story began in the 1960s, when Daniel Moynihan argued that poverty was a question of "culture."[15] By

14. Fraser, *Age of Acquiescence,* 211.
15. *Culture of poverty* is a controversial and highly criticized term, coined by anthropologist Oscar Lewis in his study of an impoverished family in Mexico City called *Children of Sanchez* (New York: Vintage, 2011). Daniel Moynihan's "The Negro Family: The Case for National Action" (March 1965) also focused on family and culture as the sources of immiseration. https://www.dol.gov/general/aboutdol/history/webid -moynihan.

the 1980s, the American middle class was terrified of falling into the classes below it, and its own financial well-being was, objectively speaking, increasingly at risk. In a new age of instability and middle-class fragility, it was hypnotized by the spectacle of the yuppies as a class above and terrified of the classes below.

The framing of such economic strife obscured its material conditions by overemphasizing culture over political economy. Fredric Jameson and other Marxists identified a "cultural turn" in our understanding of social antagonism, eclipsing economic conditions for apparatuses of divining tastes and affects. By the 1990s, the cultural rebels who had gotten PhDs in the 1970s stormed the university and secured tenured positions. They did not pay attention to budgets and administration as much as they were obsessed with their own commitments to cultural transgression, some of which involved wearing jeans to class, smoking pot, sleeping with students, and listening to John Cale, but also enjoying Madonna's MTV videos. Jean Baudrillard had taught us that everything was simulacral, and it did seem as if style had become the most important part of substance, and words become signifiers were permanently untethered from their referents. In the evolution of PMC, antagonism against mainstream culture and ordinary people were mixed up with its smug sense of subcultural superiority.

"Transgressing" the Boundaries of Professionalism

IN 1996, when *Social Text* accepted and published Alan Sokal's "Transgressing the Boundaries: Towards a Transformative Hermeneutics of Quantum Gravity," the editors believed they were publishing the work of what we would call today a "woke" physicist and mathematician. With footnotes citing theorists from Derrida to Guattari and Deleuze, Sokal made the hair-raising claim that

> deep conceptual shifts within twentieth-century science have undermined . . . Cartesian-Newtonian metaphysics; revisionist studies in the history and philosophy of science have cast further doubt on its credibility; and, most recently, feminist and post-structuralist critiques have demystified the substantive content of mainstream Western scientific practice, revealing the ideology of domination concealed behind the façade of "objectivity." It has thus become increasingly apparent that physical "reality," no less than social "reality," is at bottom a social and linguistic construct.[1]

1. Alan Sokal, "Transgressing the Boundaries: Towards a Transformative Hermeneutics of Quantum Gravity," *Social Text* 46/47 (1996): 217–52, https://physics.nyu.edu/faculty/sokal/transgress_v2 /transgress_v2_singlefile.html.

In the name of poststructural theory and the radical relativism that masked its liberal pluralism, Sokal's article denied the very foundations of modern science—that we live in a world governed by the laws of physics, which can be observed and described. Eager to support theory-friendly, anti-Enlightenment writing that allowed for the confusion of relativism with relativity, *Social Text* editors Stanley Aronowitz, Bruce Robbins, Andrew Ross and the article's peer reviewers were ready to believe that mathematics and allopathic medicine were just waiting to be disrupted and transgressed by "theory" itself. Sokal's essay on quantum physics seemed to usher in a new matriarchal multiverse governed by unstable but transgressive subatomic particles, zigzagging through reality, ready to blow our minds and bend our genders and our taste cultures.

After Sokal revealed that his article was a hoax designed to reveal the lack of intellectual and scientific standards of judgment in the top journal of cultural studies, the editors responded with condescension, outrage, and defensiveness. Sokal claimed that theory of the poststructuralist kind was a fraud, not based on academic research or evidence, and dependent on ambitious authors making the right noises about bogus bogeymen like science and objectivity. In turn, the editors of *Social Text* claimed that when they first received Sokal's submission, they thought he was a naive science guy who was worthy of encouragement, trying to master theory a bit clumsily and overzealously. After first condescending to him (by allegedly encouraging him), they demonized him when they discovered his article was a hoax. They accused Sokal of unethical behavior and bad faith. The fact was, it was the editors' mistake to have published the article. Its publication did serious damage to the reputation of the humanities, at least within the academy. Physicists and mathematicians and young scientists working in quantum physics and quantum chemistry still study the Sokal affair. Theorists and humanists tend to try to forget it. In any case, there were no professional consequences for any of the editors of the journal.[2] In fact, the reputations of Ross, Aronowitz, and Robbins were burnished in theory circles because they claimed to be fighting the good fight against the reactionary enemies of theory and identity politics. The three editors represented what would become the dominant, PMC-approved identitarian positions in academic circles. It should be noted that the Sokal affair took place during the height of the culture wars in the American academy, and theoretical and cultural studies innovators painted all opponents of their epistemological innovations as reactionaries, trying to hold on to outdated ideas like objectivity and, worse yet, universalism.

The poststructuralist cultural studies theorists despised the oppressive post–World War II liberal consensus as much as the most visionary of neoliberal economists like Alan Greenspan and his overlord, Ayn Rand. That liberal consensus was based on state and corporate support for lifetime employment, labor power, and strong social services and redistributive economic policies. The New Left/cultural studies types hated the liberal consensus as much as the neoliberals. If you do not believe me, do a search for liberal consensus in digitized copies of cultural studies books of the 1990s and you will see it appears only to be dismissed with the patriarchy and heteronormativity and a vaguely Foucauldian idea of "domination." The economic system and the social safety net built by that much despised consensus were already fragilized in the 1990s by years of corporate depredations. As Elizabeth Warren and Teresa Sullivan showed in their 2001 book *The Fragile Middle Class: Americans in Debt,* wage compression and the rising cost of living had forced the American middle class to carry debt to maintain standards of

2. https://physics.nyu.edu/faculty/sokal/SocialText_reply_LF.pdf.

living once achieved through wage growth.[3] Warren and Sullivan showed that middle-class people were unable to live on their salaries and that they were being exploited by financial instruments like credit cards and second mortgages to supplement stagnant wages. They were not going on vacations by borrowing money—they were paying medical bills, college tuition, and the costs of starting their own small businesses after being laid off or having family members laid off from stable jobs. The trends that Warren and Sullivan identified only intensified after their book was published. Economic growth had left most Americans behind, but real estate values continued to rise, despite stock market volatility in the 1990s and early 2000s. Banks discovered that middle- and working-class mortgage debt was an untapped source of profit for creditors as long as housing prices kept going up. Still suffering from wage compression, Americans used their homes for second mortgages to pay for their exploding cost of living. Banks were so eager to refinance debt and offer barely employed people credit during the early aughts: only the flimsiest forms of documentation were needed for homeowners and home buyers to get big loans. These loans would be at the heart of the subprime mortgage meltdown. People were encouraged to buy expensive new homes or refinance their paid-off homes, borrowing money at low interest rates that would balloon in a few years. The banks packaged these almost fraudulent loans, known as subprime mortgages, into complex instruments that marbled good debt and risky debt into things called collateralized debt obligations.

The house of cards came tumbling down when stressed homeowners began to default on their loans. Bear Stearns, an invest-

3. Elizabeth Warren and Teresa A. Sullivan, *The Fragile Middle Class: Americans in Debt* (New Haven, Conn.: Yale University Press, 2001).

ment bank overexposed to high-risk debt instruments, ran out of money in March 2008. Lehman Brothers went bankrupt that fall, and the stock market and the housing market crashed one after the other. Wealthy people blamed poor people for trying to cash in on a crazy market—but we know that moral failings or a "culture" of indebtedness was not the real cause of the crash. I heard wealthy Americans in my family complain that the crisis was caused by poor people buying flat-screen televisions. Once again, as they did in the Gilded Age, the wealthy found ways of feeling superior to the poor, but this time in the mode of their more virtuous handling of their wealth. Ordinary Americans, it turned out, were ensnared by a sticky web of corruption, financialization, compressed wages, fear of falling, and lack of regulation. For journalists and financial historians like John Cassidy and Adam Tooze, the crash and the ensuing bailout are directly related to the fall of centrist governments around the world.[4]

On September 10, 2008, Hank Paulson, George W. Bush's Treasury secretary, and Ben Bernanke, chairman of the Federal Reserve, went to Congress to urge lawmakers to bail out the collapsing banking sector. In 2009, under the new Obama administration, Timothy Geithner engineered TARP, or the Troubled Asset Relief Program, giving banks $700 million of public money to balance their books. According to Tooze's analysis, the Federal Reserve transferred an additional $5 trillion to non-American banks to guarantee global financial liquidity. In the meantime, between 2007 and 2016, 7.8 million Americans lost their homes to

---

4. John Cassidy offers a short and comprehensive account of the global political fallout of the 2008 crisis in the *New Yorker* on the tenth anniversary of the crash, "The Real Cost of the 2008 Financial Crisis," https://www.newyorker.com/magazine/2018/09/17/the-real-cost-of-the -2008-financial-crisis. See also Adam Tooze, *Crashed: How a Decade of Financial Crises Changed the World* (New York: Penguin, 2018).

foreclosure.[5] The economic crisis and subsequent bailout exacerbated inequality by every metric and did not lead to significant reform of the financial sector. Bailed-out banks continued to foreclose on the homes of working-class families while refusing to make new loans to creditworthy borrowers. Under an Ivy League–educated African American president, African American family wealth had collapsed. In fact, it is common knowledge that African American and Latino homeowners were hit hardest by the 2008 financial crisis: by 2018, an African American family owned $5.00 in assets for every $100.00 owned by white families.[6] Obama's identity politics did not translate into economic policies that benefited minorities and working-class people.

In the wake of the 2008 crash, and in the midst of Occupy Wall Street–generated protest excitement, John and Barbara Ehrenreich returned to their 1977 critique and declared the "death of a yuppie dream."[7] Their obituary for the yuppie was premature and overly optimistic, but they were writing at a moment when it seemed that the PMC could reinvent itself in solidarity with the working class. The Ehrenreichs, like Christopher

5. For an account of how obscure debt instruments were created and proliferated before the crisis of 2008, read Gillian Tett's *Fool's Gold: The Inside Story of J.P. Morgan and How Wall Street Greed Corrupted Its Bold Dream and Created a Financial Catastrophe* (New York: Free Press, 2010). For a more character-driven version of the crash, see Michael Lewis's *The Big Short: Inside the Doomsday Machine* (New York: W. W. Norton, 2010) and Adam McKay's film of the same name starring Christian Bale.

6. Paul Kari, "A Decade after the Housing Crisis, Foreclosures Still Haunt Homeowners," https://www.marketwatch.com/story/a-decade -after-the-housing-crisis-foreclosures-still-haunt-homeowners-2018-09 -27.

7. John Ehrenreich and Barbara Ehrenreich, *Death of a Yuppie Dream: The Rise and Fall of the Professional Managerial Class* (New York: Rosa Luxembourg Stiftung, 2013), http://www.rosalux-nyc.org/wp -content/files_mf/ehrenreich_death_of_a_yuppie_dream90.pdf.

Lasch before them, emphasized that the PMC was having difficulty reproducing itself because it had undermined working conditions for all Americans while raising too high the barrier of entry into the credentialed classes. PMC families and their children were reeling from the punishing cost of higher education as well as the narrowing gates of a corrupt meritocracy. In pinning their hopes on the Occupy Wall Street movement, the Ehrenreichs wanted to will the PMC to real political oppositionality.[8] It is undeniable that young, downwardly mobile, college-educated "occupiers" attracted national attention when protestors took over Zucotti Park on Wall Street on September 17, 2011. They were evicted two months later, but the movement articulated a durable formula for describing economic inequality: "we are the 99 percent" set up the antagonism between the 1 percent, or richest segment of the population, and the rest of us, even the top 9 percent, or those members of the PMC. A survey done by City University of New York researchers Ruth Milkman, Stephanie Luce, and Penny Lewis on May 1, 2012, during a massive protest attended by many former occupiers showed that the activists and former occupiers were mostly college-educated, white-collar professionals, majority male, with only 8 percent of occupiers/respondents reporting themselves as blue collar.[9] In their analysis of Occupy, Milkman, Luce, and Lewis emphasized the experience of the core activists, their allegiance to the Canadian anticonsumerist magazine *Adbusters,* and the inspiration they took from the Arab Spring protests.

8. Ehrenreich and Ehrenreich, 11.
9. Ruth Milkman, Stephanie Luce, and Penny Lewis, "Changing the Subject: A Bottom Up Account of Occupy Wall Street in New York City," https://www.researchgate.net/publication/268126261_Changing _The_Subject_Occupy_Wall_Street's_Achievements_and_Prospects_In _Comparative_Perspective.

One occupier quoted by Milkman, Luce, and Lewis said that "OWS [Occupy Wall Street] was a floating signifier that everybody saw different things in."[10] The idea of the floating signifier was one of the most important tenets of poststructuralist theory. It was based on the linguistic theory of Ferdinand de Saussure applied by Claude Levi-Strauss to the cultural sphere in general. For Saussure, the linguistic signifier was untethered from any referential determination to objects in the empirical world. Saussure's structuralist theory of meaning generated by difference rather than intention was highly influential in the fields of anthropology and literary theory. For Saussure, the combination of the signified (referent) and the signifier (the linguistic unit of meaning) together made up the "sign." Poststructuralism took the principles of linguistics and transferred them to philosophy, culture, and literary texts. Meaning could "float" above the signified world: signifiers became both empty and playful, detached from signifieds or referents. Puns became a form of thinking while "difference" replaced contradiction (in either Hegelian or Marxist terms) as the sinews that held together and determined flexible structures of interpretation.[11] In 1994, Alan Sokal tried to puncture the poststructuralist approach to politics and culture by showing that it was foolish to "apply" poststructural ideas to physics and scientific attempts to describe physical reality, but in 2012, students of theory were happily applying the findings of Saussurean linguistics to one of the most significant popular protest movements of the new millennium. Sokal's project failed to put any of the poststructural nostra to rest, as a generation of theory-trained young people took to the public spaces of New York City to protest a financial system that was in fact

10. Milkman, Luce, and Lewis, 25.

11. Ferdinand de Saussure, *Course in General Linguistics*, 10th ed., trans. Roy Harris (Peru, Ill.: Open Court Editions, 2011).

very compatible with floating signifiers, radical pluralism, and the untethering of financial values from empirical realities. Signs emptied of meaning gave stock brokers, financial analysts, and occupiers alike a sophisticated way of talking about value, cons, lies, and grifts.

In the same set of interviews, activist Arun Gupta talks about Ernesto Laclau and Chantal Mouffe's concept of chains of equivalence, where everyone's grievances could be seen as equal to everyone else's grievances. Laclau and Mouffe's tortured theory of populism risked no popular appeal, but it created the illusion of analyzing a "new" form of politics.[12] The highly educated members of Occupy fetishized the procedural regulation and management of discussion to reach consensus about all collective decisions. Daily meetings or General Assemblies were managed according to a technique called the progressive stack. Its fanatical commitment to proceduralism an administrative strategy suppressed real discussion of priorities or politics and ended up promoting only the integrity of the progressive stack itself. Protecting the stack became more important than formulating political demands that might have resonated with hundreds of millions of Americans whose lives were being directly destroyed by finance capital. PMC/ New Left ideas about mass movements dominated Occupy's dreams of politics and limited the effectiveness of its activism. Demographically and politically, Occupy was squarely a PMC elite formation: "Changing the Subject" is a fundamentally sympathetic account of Occupy's politics, but its demographic findings about the movement paint a stark portrait of the typical occupier, who was downwardly mobile, male, young, white, educated at an elite university, and in student loan and

12. Saussure.

credit card debt. The heavy union representation at Occupy reflected the predominance of unionized graduate students.

By 2016, PMC elites became even more worshipful of money and more contemptuous of ordinary people: Hillary Clinton as a successor to Barack Obama was the incarnation of PMC values and the Democratic Party's power elite. Under Hillary Clinton, the Democratic Party would no longer concern itself with working-class interests, the ones her husband had ignored despite his good old boy style: the exercise of power would consist of protecting capitalism while setting up a carefully groomed lineup of diverse, donor-friendly candidates to run for the highest offices in the land. Wall Street and Silicon Valley donors would be appeased. No one to her left dared to challenge her run, except for Bernie Sanders, senator from Vermont. Clinton was the PMC elite's dream candidate, a sign that the class had completely taken over the once unruly Democratic Party that had formerly represented working-class interests. Clinton was an alleged shoo-in, the most qualified presidential candidate ever, a woman who loved Wall Street and the ruling class, a Lean-in pseudo-feminist who wanted to inspire girls to become *girl bosses.* Clinton's defeat was not just a blow to centrist rule; it was an angry rejection of the hypocrisy of the PMC *tout court.* Because of the rise of right-wing populism, political commentators were forced to deal with the election in terms of class formation, which they quickly transformed into geographical and cultural differences that divided America and needed to be understood as such.

From the 1990s, transgressive antiprofessionalism had become the opium of the vanguard corps of PMC elites. Angela Nagle's book *Kill All Normies: On Line Culture Wars from 4Chan and Tumblr to Trump and the Alt-Right* angered these cultural studies transgression worshippers. Like Sokal, Nagle is a proponent of the Old Left, but unlike Sokal, she was not a tenured professor in a STEM field. Nagle has been cancelled by scholars writing the kinds of things that Sokal parodied. Liberal academics could not bear to see their love of subcultural insider knowledge questioned or criticized, especially by an adjunct and junior scholar.[13] Since the publication of Nagle's book, which was critical of her work, Gabriella Coleman, holder of the Wolf Chair in Scientific and Technological Literacy at McGill University, has worked tirelessly to blacklist and deplatform the Irish scholar. Nagle, who worked for years as an adjunct and journalist in the para-academic world, has little institutional power or standing in comparison with Coleman, the prize-winning ethnographer of Anonymous. Nagle suggested that Coleman's 2014 book *Hacker, Hoaxer, Whistleblower, Spy* was one example of the feverish academic embrace of transgression and its antinormie animus. Nagle argues in passing that Coleman lost her distance to her ethnographic subjects of study—Internet provocateurs like /weev/, Andrew Aurenheimer, convicted and sentenced in 2012 of hacking AT&T. Coleman loves transgression, the kind parodied by Sokal, and her book is rife with gushing accounts of her relationships with online microcelebrities.[14] Coleman is unfazed by the fact that /weev/ turned out to be an anti-Semitic, neo-Nazi webmaster of the far right website Daily Stormer. In contrast to Coleman, Nagle argued that the Left should be embracing the normative forces of class struggle, not the subcultural transgressions and exploits of people like Aurenheimer. Nagle believes in mass, working-class-based coalitions and movements, not subcultural fetish politics, which she finds undermines the

13. Angela Nagle, *Kill All Normies: On Line Culture Wars from 4Chan and Tumblr to Trump and the Alt-Right* (London: Zero Books, 2017).

14. Gabriella Coleman, *Hacker, Hoaxer, Whistleblower, Spy: The Many Faces of Anonymous* (London: Verso, 2014).

forms of solidarity that are needed for the long struggles of the future. Parody, civil dissent, reasoned debate, contradiction, and polemics are useless, however, against people who see the world as a series of opportunities for transgressing boundaries and celebrating floating signifiers and Deleuzian lines of flight.

In fact, Sokal's and Nagel's object of critique—the academic fetish for the transgression of "norms"—has become a "progressive" PMC elite strategy for gaining media attention. With the help of private foundations that are tireless in promoting their antiworker, antiacademic freedom agenda, today's academic entrepreneurs are using social causes to further their own agendas. Academic research, at least in the humanities and social sciences, is being subtly shaped by the agendas of the ruling class—sometimes directly by mega-wealthy individuals, but also by private foundations endowed by mega-wealthy individuals, and their liberal-minded employees in para-academic positions in the media. It's not even clear that these professionals and opportunists understand the part they're playing in undermining academic freedom or professional autonomy.

Take, for example, the role a once obscure private foundation, the Pulitzer Center, played in catapulting the 1619 Project into the center of the national debate about race, slavery, and the teaching and framing of American history. The Pulitzer Center allegedly "raises awareness of underreported global issues through direct support of quality journalism across all media platforms and a unique program of education and public outreach." The Pulitzer Center's most prolific donor is Emily Rauh Pulitzer and the Emily Rauh Pulitzer Foundation. Widow of newspaperman Joseph Pulitzer, Rauh Pulitzer is also a major donor to the arts.

In 2019, the Pulitzer Center collaborated with the *New York Times Magazine* to launch the 1619 Project, directed by journalist Nikole Hannah-Jones. The Project was launched to commemorate the four-hundredth anniversary of the arrival of the first enslaved peoples in the American colonies—for its collaborators, the real birthday of the United States of America. Included as part of the *New York Times Magazine* in August 2019, the 1619 Project caused quite a media sensation: copies of the Sunday *Times* in which it was included quickly sold out. The Project rewrites the American revolution as a revolt of slaveholders against the British abolitionists and, in its first iteration, argues that the United States of America should be understood as first and foremost a country founded in defense of the institution of slavery. Against the historical evidence that the British monarchy was not taking anti–Atlantic slave trade positions before 1776 and that the colonists themselves were divided on the issue, Hannah-Jones leads a group of writers, scholars, and journalists to dismiss the work of historians of colonial America in order to promote their view of the nation as hopelessly and exceptionally racist.

Just as the editors of *Social Text* and their colleagues were happy to transgress the norms of the scientific and mathematical communities two decades ago, the 1619 Project rejects the norms of historical research. In the case of the 1619 Project, however, the *New York Times* is not a small academic journal: the fear of offending the powerful forces, funders and donors who support the Project through private foundations, has cast a pall over the debate around its findings. The authors of the Project reject all criticism of it: they believe that their findings do not depend on the research consensus and archival evidence sorted through by a scholarly community of historians. Using her new clout and massive audience, Nikole Hannah-Jones led the way in dismissing the accepted scholarship that had been done on colonial America as simply the highly biased work of white males. Lifetimes of careful, empirical research were simply no match for massive foundation dollars backed by one of the largest media companies in the world.

It is clear that powerful financial and media interests are behind the promotion of the 1619 Project and its bold attempt to change the way we understand American history and historical research itself. The Project is on top of everything, a bold attempt to eliminate historical materialism from the teaching and writing of American history while destroying the possibility of solidarity in the American working class. Socialist historians on the pages of the World Socialist Web Site (WSWS.org) have been some of the Project's most vocal and astute critics, but their work is not supported or funded by a dense and tangled network of foundations and media elites.[15] The Project wants to lay out a subtle but clear lesson for its readers: the impossibility of working-class solidarity. The World Socialist Web Site is also one of the few media outlets to have publicized the fact that under pressure from historians, the *New York Times* and Hannah-Jones have quietly abandoned their initial claims that 1619 was the "true founding moment" of the United States. Rather than publish a retraction or a correction of their claim, they have quietly softened their thesis on the website of the project by claiming that the Project's goal is about centering slavery and the contributions of black Americans in relationship to American identity and narrativized nationhood.[16] No trace of the earlier hyperbolic claims remains on the 1619

15. For an overview of the Project and the responses it evoked, see https://www.nytimes.com/interactive/2019/08/14/magazine/1619 -america-slavery.html; https://www.theatlantic.com/ideas/archive/2020 /01/1619-project-new-york-times-wilentz/605152/; https://www.wsws .org/en/articles/2019/09/06/1619-s06.html?mod=article_inline.

16. Tom Mackaman and David North, "The New York Times and Nikole Hannah-Jones Abandon Key Claims of the 1619 Project," World Socialist Website, September 22, 2020, https://www.wsws.org/en /articles/2020/09/22/1619-s22.html.

Project website, but researchers at WSWS.org retained a copy of the original site's thesis about the founding the United States.

Few stop to ask why such powerful and affluent donors and organizations would be so invested in such a historical project—particularly one that elicited such strong counterarguments from widely respected historians. In its focus on race and the singularity of the history of American slavery, the 1619 Project ignores historical and economic conditions that might make slavery comparable to other forms of exploitation—chattel slavery and serfdom being two premodern examples and the wage slavery of industrial capitalism being another. In doing so, it furthers a cherished liberal rallying cry of our time: that interracial solidarity among the working class is simply impossible—better not even to try to establish a universalist critique of capitalism. The leading thinkers of the 1619 Project insist that it is race, not class, that has created the essential social and economic fault line in America. Racism is, they argue, a transhistorical fact written into our national character.

This view fits in nicely with the story of American pluralism promoted by postwar private foundation–sponsored ideology. From a pluralist point of view, African Americans are a distinctive and powerful interest group who, because of their particular history, should advocate for themselves and for reparations for the singular suffering they endured under the particularly brutal institution of American slavery—there's no need for them to join labor unions with other workers whose experiences can never be a perfect match for their own. Other "groups," Hispanics, Latinos, Asian Americans, Native Americans, and so on, can each advocate separately for their special interests. They just need to come up with competing versions of their historical singularity and find powerful donors who will support them in publicizing their cause.

In the early 1970s, just as the policies of deindustrialization and austerity were being perfected as instruments of class warfare in the United States, Jonathan Cobb and Richard Sennett interviewed the janitor "Ricca Kartides" (a pseudonym) for *The Hidden Injuries of Class*. The young sociologists discovered that Kartides, who worked as a janitor, felt humiliated every day by his job and its low social status. He was, however, on his salary alone, able to buy his own home so that his children wouldn't have to live in the building he cleaned. Kartides's ability to buy a house and support a family on his wages is unimaginable today.[17] Today, the average janitor, who makes $24,000 a year, may be ostensibly or formally equal to the average CEO, who makes $14 million a year, but that equality seems like a cruel joke played by capitalism and liberal democracy on the working class.

The radical and material difference in average income between janitor and CEO should be intolerable to everyone who is not a capitalist, but PMC elites have internalized the values of the meritocracy so deeply that they cannot see the radical nature of this difference in incomes as essentially different from all other kinds of difference. As social and economic stratification intensifies across the globe, it spawns a series of political crises and shocks that have shaken centrist governments that have promoted neoliberal, austerity-driven policies for the past fifty years. It is in the face of such a destabilized polity and an ongoing political and economic crisis that a renewed Left must produce political critique and a cultural program informed by the needs of mass politics. If the Left refuses to produce better, more historically grounded accounts of the past, ones that situate contemporary class and cultural conflict in the context of historical struggles for universal principles of equality, dignity,

17. Richard Sennett and Jonathan Cobb, *The Hidden Injuries of Class* (New York: W. W. Norton, 1972).

and emancipation, liberals will not do it for us. Liberals have abandoned history, because they have to believe they are superior to elites of the past and the contemporary working class at the same time. Members of the PMC believe themselves to be virtuous vanguardists, floating above historical forms and conditions, transgressing boundaries and inventing new ways of being and seeing. It is hard to argue with them, because they do not accept debate as a meaningful form of the advancement of knowledge. For them, every conflict is moral, not intellectual or political. Sokal failed to stop the proliferation of Americanized ahistorical poststructuralist lines of research in the humanities. Nagel reframed the notion of transgression, but found herself banished from academia. I have no illusions about the power of my critique against the dominant tendencies in academia today, but I will not stop criticizing opportunistic forms of antihistorical, and antimaterialist, antiprofessional work in my profession.

The PMC Has Children

FROM THE VERY MOMENT OF CONCEPTION, which for PMC parents is always a "choice," the future child and infant possesses "potential" that has to be both optimized and maximized. PMC mothers have to do prenatal yoga while setting up intra-uterine Mozart streams on pregnant bellies. Preparing for a child is just the beginning of a torturous and expensive preoccupation for today's elites.[1] PMC people are both terrified of and thrilled by procreation, because children cannot help but amplify social anxieties about competition. For Paula Fass, fear is one of the distinctive features of contemporary middle-class parenting, as middle-class parents "imagine what an unsuccessful child might face in the future."[2] Even with full-time hired help, PMC working parents are stressed about infant pedagogy and proper stimulation while pulling down the double salaries that allow them to maintain upper-middle-class consumption habits.[3] Babies

1. Paula Fass, *The End of American Childhood: A History of Parenting from Life on the Frontier to the Managed Child* (Princeton, N.J.: Princeton University Press, 2016), 222–23.
2. Fass, 222.
3. Elizabeth Warren and Amalia Warren Tyagi, *The Two Income Trap: Why Middle Class Families Are (Still) Going Broke* (New York: Basic Books, 2016).

are notoriously sensual beings, both dependent and hedonistic. Their helplessness and drive for pleasure represent an existential threat to the Puritanism of American elites. It is not surprising, then, that managing the development of children into successful adults dominates the ethos of PMC parenting. For them, the 40 percent of American children conceived outside of marriage and the upper middle class are deemed unworthy of collective attention or public concern. You don't have to be a socialist to see the reproduction of class privilege played out in the most dramatic and extreme ways in childcare, children's health, and children's education.

In her best seller *Perfect Madness: Motherhood in an Age of Anxiety*, Judith Warner decries the anguished, competitive perfectionism of contemporary upper-middle-class motherhood.[4] Since Warner published her book in 2006, the anxiety she describes has only intensified. Megan Erickson argues that these anxieties and fears are not unjustified, "given the increasing stratification even within the top 1% of the country's earners as the 2008–2009 financial crisis has only exacerbated the class war that those on top wage against all those below them."[5] Parenting fads have become hot commodities in America's wealthiest neighborhoods. Perfectionist PMC parents are crusading class formation pioneers: they will not hesitate to humiliate nannies, babysitters, teachers, grandmothers, and other parents about the horrific effects of vaccines, screen time, tickling, dolls with faces, video games, cigarette-shaped candy, or sugar in general. With COVID-19, children of the wealthiest Americans who are enrolled in private schools enjoy full-time private tutors and

4. Judith Warner, *Perfect Madness: Motherhood in the Age of Anxiety* (New York: Penguin, 2004).

5. Megan Erickson Kilpatrick, *Class War: The Privatization of Childhood* (London: Verso, 2015).

smaller class sizes on Zoom and/or in person, mitigating risk and maximizing stimulation and education.

Around 1900, the emerging PMC became concerned with children's welfare from a public policy standpoint. As Judith Sealander notes, social reform movements promoted a powerful vision of the role of government in redressing social ills, especially when it came to childcare and maternal health. But as the twentieth century came to an end, PMC elites became fully neoliberalized and joined their voices to the right-wing denunciation of "big government" and its allegedly debilitating "handouts."[6] Bill Clinton's Personal Responsibility and Work Opportunity Act of 1996, or welfare reform, inaugurated a relentless war against the youngest, the poorest, and the most vulnerable people in the country. To qualify for welfare, the poorest American mother had to find a job and keep it, even though she could not afford childcare on her meager salary. Austerity and "personal responsibility" have been the sigils under which benefit-cutting austerity policies were forged to torture those who had the least in an affluent society. In the United States, there is always enough for tax cuts for the rich and never enough money for social programs for children and their caretakers. In matters of child welfare, the PMC elite believe that the social surplus, or surplus value generated by the totality of economic activity, should be enjoyed by the children of the wealthy few, while the majority of working-class and working-poor children and their caretakers are consigned to lives of punishment, surveillance, and parsimonious rewards.

In his enduring best seller *Baby and Child Care,* first published in 1945 as the baby boomers were taking their first baby steps, Benjamin Spock advised anxious postwar parents to trust

6. Judith Sealander, *The Failed Century of the Child: Governing America's Young in the Twentieth Century* (Cambridge: Cambridge University Press, 2003).

themselves with their babies.[7] Dr. Spock became one of the most influential experts in child-rearing for post–World War II America. Popularizing psychoanalytic ideas about pleasure and projection, he played a critical role in the formation of new PMC identities. Spock advocated against traditional ideas about infant discipline and told young, newly prosperous blue- and white-collar parents to trust themselves with their babies. Despite the fact that Spock warned parents against faddish child-rearing counsel, his own advice was packaged in a popular book that has been hailed as the American twentieth century's second best seller, after the Bible. Dr. Spock was also an outspoken, anti–Vietnam War, New Left activist. Conservatives blamed him for fomenting countercultural revolt and encouraging young people to be self-indulgent rebels since their Dr. Spock–reading parents had not disciplined them as infants. His advice, however, had a paradoxical tone, familiar to consumers of self-help literature. Dr. Spock reminded his readers relentlessly that *they* were the ones in the know. "You can read books and articles, but the main way you will learn is to be observant in a meaningful way. That means spending time, looking and listening to your baby, not just feeding and cleaning him … and then trusting yourself. Because you *do* know more than you do."[8]

In the 1970s, as budding PMC boomers dabbled in "Eastern" religions, privileged self-exploration over tradition, and pursued emotional and sexual experimentation, they looked at the working class as out-of-touch authoritarians who married for life and lived in traditional two-parent families. Today, after decades of austerity, working-class families and kinship networks are at a

7. Benjamin Spock, *Dr. Spock's Baby and Childcare*, 9th ed. (New York: Pocket Books, 2011).

8. Benjamin Spock, *Dr. Spock's "The First Two Years"* (New York: Pocket Books, 2001).

breaking point. Jefferson Cowie and Jennifer Silva have shown that working-class Americans today have more unstable family lives and greater instances of divorce and single parenthood than their PMC counterparts.[9] PMC people are far more likely to marry and remain married. They rarely if ever marry outside their class. The PMC family has become a veritable redoubt from which class privilege is reproduced, but with stingy parental leave policies, increasing health care costs, compressed wages, and the exploding cost of higher education, the PMC family feels beleaguered and threatened by the possibility of failing to raise the most "successful" children. In the time of COVID-19, these anxieties have not gone away. They have been exacerbated.

In 2014, Yale Law School faculty members Amy Chua and Jed Rubenfeld proved Marx right by publishing *The Triple Package: How Three Unlikely Traits Explain the Rise and Fall of Cultural Groups in America,* a book that was purely determined by the "material life conditions" of its authors.[10] After the runaway success of 2011's *Battle Hymn of the Tiger Mother,* a best-selling parenting memoir about Chua's attempts to optimize her daughters' childhoods and childhood activities, Tina Bennett, Chua's literary agent, no doubt hoped for a follow-up volume that would fly off the shelves like the first book.[11] Chua's best seller was an irritating but highly entertaining read. When the *Wall Street Journal* excerpted a part of *Battle Hymn* under the title "Why

9. Jefferson Cowie, *Stayin' Alive: The 1970s and the Last Days of the Working Class* (New York: New Press, 2010), and Jennifer Silva, *Coming Up Short: Working Class Adulthood in an Age of Uncertainty* (Oxford: Oxford University Press, 2013).

10. Amy Chua and Jed Rubenfeld, *The Triple Package: How Three Unlikely Traits Explain the Rise and Fall of Cultural Groups in America* (New York: Penguin, 2015).

11. Amy Chua, *Battle Hymn of the Tiger Mother* (New York: Penguin, 2011).

Chinese Mothers Are Superior," the Tiger Mother brand hit pay dirt.[12] Despite her repeated protestations that her book and its title were both self-disparaging and self-reflexive, readers took her memoir as a parenting how-to guide.

Chua and Rubenfeld argued in perfect matrimonial sync that successful "cultural groups" have the triple package: (1) a superiority complex, (2) an inferiority complex, and—wait for it—(3) better impulse control. This last quality, famously (and falsely) lacking in those who happen to be African American, Mexican American, or just poor, explains why groups that do not defer satisfaction fail to "succeed." Chua and Rubenfeld offer repackaged social Darwinist–tinged, culture-of-poverty arguments that are trotted out every few years to justify the entrenched immiseration of large swathes of the American population. Who are successful in America, according to the two Yale law professors, one now disgraced? A narrow band of wealthy meritocrats, of course. In Chua and Rubenfeld's United States, there is no polity, no class, no society, no collective endeavor, no social responsibility: there are only "cultural groups" vying for advantages in the fields of prestige and business. Their idea of a better world? The abolition of the whole idea of a "group." America will be a better place when there are only successful and unsuccessful individuals, all competing on an allegedly even playing field.

Despite Rubenfeld's apparent professional "success," he has proven himself woefully lacking in impulse control. In August 2020, Rubenfeld was quietly suspended from Yale Law School for sexual misconduct, including predatory and harassing behavior toward female students.[13] Recently, Yale Law School

12. Amy Chua, "Why Chinese Mothers Are Superior," *Wall Street Journal,* January 8, 2011, https://www.wsj.com/articles/SB10001424052748704111504576059713528698754.

13. Mihir Zaveri, "Yale Law Professor Is Suspended after Sexual

students have demanded his permanent removal. A group of students is petitioning the president of Yale, Peter Salovey, to have Rubenfeld permanently removed from the faculty.[14]

As the gulf between rich and poor has widened, while social mobility has decreased in every racial and ethnic group, the PMC home has become a laboratory of increasingly lavish and expensive childcare equipment and demanding child-rearing techniques that now include outright bribes and elaborate cheating strategies to help their children succeed at any cost. The Varsity Blues case, which revealed that rich and super-rich parents were paying college counselor Rick Singer hundreds of thousands of dollars to get their children through the "side door" of athletic admission into college, is only the logical outcome of ruling-class determination to guarantee their children's "success."[15]

The class war from above has had dire consequences for all American children and their caretakers, but the toll it has taken on the poorest families is staggering. Recently, the Urban Institute found that children are the poorest segment of American society, with 22 percent of American children living in poverty, while 38.8 percent of American children have experienced some form

Harassment Inquiry," *New York Times,* August 24, 2020, https://www .nytimes.com/2020/08/26/nyregion/jed-rubenfeld-yale.html.

14. Julia Brown, "Law Students Demand Rubenfeld's Permanent Removal, Greater Transparency," *Yale Daily News,* October 12, 2020, https://yaledailynews.com/blog/2020/10/12/law-students-demand -rubenfelds-permanent-removal-greater-transparency/.

15. The Varsity Blues case involved Rick Singer, college counselor to the wealthy, including actors, heiresses, and captains of industry, who all paid him to doctor test results and athletic records to gain admission for their less-than-successful progeny. For a brief summary of the college admissions scandals, see https://www.nytimes.com/2019/03/12/us /college-admissions-cheating-scandal.html.

of poverty in their lives. The numbers for African American children are even more grim, with 38.8 percent of African American children living in poverty and 75.4 percent of African children having lived in poverty.[16]

While PMC parenting books promote the extraordinary measures to which elite parents will go to guarantee their children's "success," D. W. Winnicott praised *ordinary* devoted mothers for bonding with their infants in a way that gave an astonishing majority of human beings the mental health to be able to enjoy play, creativity, and richness of experience. Winnicott had an expansive, gender-neutral idea of the caretaker; however, for the sake of brevity, I use his term the "good enough mother" in discussing his ideas.[17] In learning to take care of an infant, the "good enough mother" loves her baby but responds imperfectly to its needs; a good enough, but not perfect, caretaker begins to adapt to her baby's growing physical and emotional capacity to endure frustration by sometimes failing to respond immediately to the baby's demands. These necessary failures reflect the mother's absorption in other tasks and represent opportunities for the baby to establish a healthy tolerance for frustration as well as an incipient recognition of self and other.

In his introduction to *The Child, the Family and the Outside World,* published in 1964, Winnicott writes,

> I am trying to draw attention to the immense contribution to the individual and the society which the ordinary good mother with

---

16. Caroline Ratcliffe, *Child Poverty and Adult Success* (Washington, D.C.: Urban Institute, September 2015), https://www .urban.org/sites/default/files/publication/65766/2000369-Child -Poverty-and-Adult-Success.pdf.

17. D. W. Winnicott, *Playing and Reality* (New York: Basic Books, 1971). See also Winnicott, "Transitional Objects and Transitional Phenomena," *International Journal of Psychoanalysis* 34 (1953): 89–97.

her husband in support makes at the beginning, and which she does simply through being devoted to her infant. Is not this contribution of the devoted mother unrecognized precisely because it is immense? If this contribution is accepted it follows that everyone who is sane, everyone feels himself to be a person in the world, and for whom the world means something, every happy person, is in infinite debt to a woman. . . . The result of such recognition of the maternal role . . . will not be gratitude or even praise. The result will be a lessening in ourselves of a fear. If our society delays making full acknowledgment of this dependence which is a historical fact in the initial stage of development in every individual, there must remain a block to ease and complete health, a block that comes from a fear.[18]

It is clear from this passage that Winnicott believes that the care of infants is a social and public good to which each caretaker contributes in an infant's earliest days. Caretakers cannot be parsimonious in their gifts of love and sacrifice of sleep and libido to the dependent infant: their generosity provides the child with an inalienable legacy of security and fearlessness when facing the challenges of growing up in an uncertain world. The stressed and deprived caretaker who demands repayment or calculates the debt of a child is one who instills fear and anxiety, a state that our present-day world, made by fiscal austerity and economic sadism, knows only too well.

Although it is difficult to imagine a time when the richness of childhood experience was embraced as a public good, it was only sixty years ago that Winnicott built his psychoanalytic theories on the idea of collective and mutual responsibility for dependents and their caretakers. Winnicott's 1964 optimism about overcoming fearfulness should be both inspiring and worrying for us today when fear of falling and fear of failing seem to be

18. D. W. Winnicott, *The Child, the Family and the Outside World* (Cambridge, Mass.: Perseus, 1984), 10.

generalized conditions. In postwar Great Britain, Winnicott welcomed the redistribution of social surplus that would allow the greatest number of Britons to experience the richness and health of his own privileged childhood. He admits openly that his happy childhood allowed him to expand upon his ability for observation, empathy, and play. These qualities and abilities are part of a human legacy that every baby on the planet deserves to enjoy. Winnicott always argued that the support of a baby's caretaker is a social and collective responsibility. The unglamorous infrastructural support of good enough parenting is the good enough state, a social democratic system of redistributive support for those people who take care of the neediest and most helpless human beings. If the good enough mother can be cherished as a cultural and collective inheritance and social good, we can begin to build a society where dependency is not feared or demonized. We can begin to build a world where happy parents and stable childhoods are a collective good and no child will ever be "fine-tuned" to "succeed."

The PMC Reads a Book

ON JANUARY 16, 2017, to ready its readers for the shock of the Trump inauguration, the *New York Times* published Michiko Kakutani's portrait of Barack Obama. The "reader-in-chief," Obama was the sainted apotheosis of the PMC elite. He did not enjoy inherited wealth; he was a man of the people, found and promoted by the meritocracy. He was liberalism's dream come true. If we believed in him, then we could believe that social mobility was a "solution" to racism and inequality.

When Obama's heir apparent, Hillary Clinton, lost the 2016 election to Donald Trump, *Times* readers needed solace. The *Times* delivered. "Not since Lincoln has there been a president as fundamentally shaped in his life, convictions and outlook on the world by reading and writing as Barack Obama." In Obama's own words, reading allowed him to "slow down" and put himself in "someone else's shoes."[1] Obama was paraphrasing Atticus Finch, hero of *To Kill a Mockingbird*. In Harper Lee's award-winning novel about a lynching in Maycomb, Alabama, that took place during the Depression, Atticus teaches his daughter Jean

---

1. "Transcript: Obama on What Books Mean to Him," *New York Times,* January 16, 2017, https://www.nytimes.com/2017/01/16/books /transcript-president-obama-on-what-books-mean-to-him.html.

Louise/Scout and readers a critical lesson about literature and empathy: "You never understand a person until you consider things from his point of view . . . until you climb into his skin and walk around in it." For Obama, as for most liberal readers, that metaphorical walk takes place through the act of reading. At the end of the Obama presidency, we were bombarded with studies about how reading literature expanded our capacity for understanding the experiences of others. Atticus and Obama showed us that individual acts of empathy and private self-cultivation would produce justice and understanding in a world torn apart by racism and violence. For liberals, this narrative was reassuring: Atticus was not just genteel and antiracist but he was the most virtuous member of his community and a member of the PMC. As a country lawyer, Atticus also became the ethical center of a barbaric and racist world.

In 2010, on the fiftieth anniversary of the novel's publication, NPR celebrated Harper Lee's fiction with a frothy article in praise of the book: one of the interviewees made sure to emphasize that Oprah Winfrey called *To Kill a Mockingbird* "our national novel."[2] In the 1970s, *To Kill a Mockingbird* was an embarrassing curiosity of Cold War propaganda, but in the Obama administration's Common Core curriculum for ninth-grade language arts, *To Kill a Mockingbird* once again occupied pride of place in the canon and tradition of post–World War II American literature. The Obama administration wanted to revive the early 1960s era of high liberalism, but in style only. Although Obama had the opportunity, especially in his first term, to invest new federal funds into public education, his administration was reluctant to match the mobilization that took place in 1959, when the USSR's launch of Sputnik forced Americans to match Soviet

2. "'Mockingbird' Moments: 'Scout, Atticus and Boo,'" NPR, https://www.npr.org/templates/story/story.php?storyId=128387104.

investment in both science (STEM) research and the humanities. Obama's Common Core curriculum was allegedly a smarter set of federal standards imposed by a well-educated president to reform the dumbed-down, standardized test–oriented federal education reform instituted by his predecessor, George W. Bush, in the form of No Child Left Behind. Obama's educational reforms, however, did not spur a massive reinvestment in public schools and public universities.

As both Diane Ravitch and Megan Kilpatrick have argued, educational reform is a euphemism for an ongoing war against unionized workers and the lower ranks of white-collar professionals.[3] Fomenting public panic about the state of American schools, educational reformers, supported by for-profit corporations and not-for-profit private foundations, set out to create new assessment regimes to reward and punish teachers with merit pay and austerity budgets. For the past four decades, politicians have been trotting out the "schools are failing our children" as high neoliberal strategy in their antiworker rhetoric, attacking unionized public school teachers by undermining job security and their creative and intellectual autonomy in their classrooms. Improvement of educational outcomes for students is directly related to teacher compensation, smaller class sizes, and adequate funding, but under the Clinton, G. Bush, G. W. Bush, and Obama administrations, education reform has been designed to punish teachers for poor student performance. It is no accident that school teachers' union strikes from Chicago to West Virginia were the first signs that workers were not going to

---

3. Diane Ravitch, *The Death and Life of the Great American School System: How Testing and Choice Are Undermining Education* (New York: Basic Books, 2011); Ravitch, *Reign of Error: The Hoax of the Privatization Movement and the Danger to America's Public Schools* (New York: Vintage, 2014); Kilpatrick, *Class War*.

put up with austerity policies any longer. In recent years, teachers' strikes and their organized advocacy for their communities and their students provided some small signs of hope in labor action during times of ideological chaos.[4] Let's not forget that in the 1980s, Bill Clinton made national waves by courageously "standing up" to teachers' unions, which became a part of the centrist politicians' playbook to curry favor with conservtives. As governor of Arkansas, Clinton listened to think tank elites and proposed raising educational standards without raising school budgets. To improve Arkansas's educational attainment ranking at forty-eighth out of fifty states, Clinton imposed a standards test on teachers. In return for passing the required teacher testing as law, Clinton pushed through a slight tax increase.[5] The Heritage Foundation had found that Arkansas citizens' lawsuits to maintain per-student funding levels at $5,400 was a sign of public profligacy that needed to be tamed.[6] Bill Clinton agreed. Inciting moral panic about the state of public education has been a political expedient for liberals and conservatives alike. Bill Clinton's unique style was able to combine post-1968 institutionalized identity politics with a fervor for austerity and budget cutting that made the wealthiest Democratic Party donors as happy as their Republican counterparts.

In 2011, *Harvard Business Review* called for federal curriculum reform that would encourage creativity, complexity, cu-

4. Zacarhy B. Wolf, "Why Teachers Strikes Are Touching Every Part of America," CNN, February 23, 2019, https://edition.cnn.com/2019 /02/23/politics/teacher-strikes-politics/index.html.

5. William E. Schmidt, "Arkansas Skills Test," *New York Times,* January 17, 1984.

6. Gary W. Ritter, *Education Reform in Arkansas: Past and Present. Reforming Education in Arkansas: Recommendations from the Koret Task Force* (Stanford, Calif.: Hoover Institution Press, 2005), http://www .korettaskforce.org/books/arkansas/27.pdf.

riosity, and collaboration.[7] Shortly thereafter, then president Obama hired Yale literature major David Coleman, an assessment "expert" with an "interest" in underserved populations, to oversee the reinvigoration of the language arts requirements in the Common Core. Obama and Coleman were interested, like all educational reformers, in "raising standards." Their way of doing it? Through a program branded Race to the Top (RTT), which included the usual assessment (testing) of students and concomitant budgetary rewards and punishments for schools and teachers. Whatever the effectiveness of Common Core and RTT in raising educational attainment standards, the Obama administration left 19.3 percent of American children under the age of five living in extreme poverty.[8] Coleman left his government position to become grand master of the meritocracy, or CEO of the College Board, the highly profitable "nonprofit" organization that oversees the SATs, GREs, and MCATs and all the multiple-choice exams that are meant to predict future academic success of test takers by sorting them into ordinary and extraordinary students.

7. Adam Richardson, "Where No Child Left Behind Went Wrong," *Harvard Business Review,* October 27, 2011, https://hbr.org/2011/10 /where-no-child-left-behind-wen.

8. "Child Poverty in America 2017: National Analysis," Children's Defense Fund, https://www.childrensdefense.org/wp-content/uploads /2018/09/Child-Poverty-in-America-2017-National-Fact-Sheet.pdf. According to a recent study by the Brookings Institution, for the 16 percent of American children living in poverty, COVID-19 has escalated the emotional damage and educational deprivation from pandemic-exacerbated financial, food, and housing insecurity. Lisa A. Gennetian and Kathy Hirsh-Pasek, "Where's the Rallying Cry: America's Children Are Unequally Prepared to Absorb the Impact of COVID-19," Brookings Institution, May 13, 2020, https://www.brookings.edu/blog/education -plus-development/2020/05/13/wheres-the-rallying-cry-americas -children-are-unequally-prepared-to-absorb-the-impacts-of-covid-19/.

Coleman, like every other Obama appointee, brought a brilliant pedigree to the administration. Like every literature and English major at Yale (including the author of this book and past and future National Security Agency/Central Intelligence Agency agents, such as super-spy James Jesus Angleton), Coleman was indoctrinated with the idea that close reading is the highest form of human intellectual activity.[9] The Yale literature departments produced and promoted the Cold War based, New Criticism fetish of untangling complex texts: its fundamental methodology relied on the denial of context, whether social, historical, or political. Only under the myopic scrutiny of a good, close reading would an obdurate, clam-like text give up its iridescent pearl of gorgeous meaning. Yale and New Critics hated vulgarity and simplification in any form. Under Coleman, Common Core was shaped by the demands of close reading. When Common Core instituted a new federal test for language arts, the formidable DBQ, document-based questions, bore all the hallmarks of Yale-brewed "close readings." The problem was that DBQ were not questions at all. In the case of *To Kill a Mockingbird,* students were expected to provide document-based evidence for a carefully pre-prepared thesis. (My son was told to show how the novel argues for the importance of "taking a stand.")

So the answer would be that Atticus Finch appears as the one person in Maycomb capable of standing up to racists and rabid dogs: he is the bringer of a civilizing violence meant to protect and seal the community of the righteous. Lee's novel is filled with hatred of the angry, defiant, pleasure-seeking poor white people represented by the awful Ewells. Burris Ewell, the youngest son of that accursed family, arrives at school covered in lice. Burris's

9. Robin Winks, *Cloak and Gown: Scholars in the Secret War* (New York: Morrow, 1987); Jefferson Morely, *Ghost: The Secret Life of CIA Spymaster James Jesus Angleton* (New York: St. Martin's, 2018).

sister Mayella also has serious personal hygiene issues and is sexually needy and dishonest; the father of this accursed clan, Bob Ewell, cannot control his impulses for sex, revenge, or violence. Not surprisingly, the Ewells also live on public assistance. Bob assaults his daughter and frames African American Tom Robinson for the crime. Mayella perjures herself in court and accuses Robinson, a man she desired, of the violence inflicted upon her by her father. Atticus successfully defends Robinson in court, but Robinson is convicted despite the exculpating evidence. After his conviction, a mob lynches him while he tries to escape imprisonment. At the end of the novel, Bob Ewell is still angry about Finch's defense of the innocent man, so he tries to kill the two younger Finches. During his attempt at double homicide, he is conveniently murdered by town shut-in Boo Radley.

In the opening scene of the novel, the Cunninghams, poor, noble farmers and foils to the yucky Ewells, pay Atticus's legal fees in hickory nuts. When Scout asks Atticus if the Finches are poor, Atticus tells Scout that the Finches are poor, but not as poor as the Cunninghams. Atticus explains to Scout that the "proud" Cunninghams, whose farm is mortgaged to the hilt, will not take public assistance. The Cunninghams are virtuous poor people. The Ewells are bad poor people: they take public help. With more than half of American children having experienced public assistance at some point or another in their short lives, it seems sadistic to make them read a novel about a noble, virtuous lawyer and the evil public assistance–abusing poor people trying to kill his family. If poor ninth graders pay attention in their language arts classes, they must feel humiliated by their family's willingness to take what the worthy poor of Harper Lee's novel refuse.[10]

10. https://www.thoughtco.com/who-really-receives-welfare -41265.

It is clear that the ideological message of *To Kill a Mockingbird* underwrote Bill Clinton's 1996 welfare reform. Just as Clinton attacked teachers when he was governor of Arkansas, he attacked welfare and welfare recipients as president. In creating more punishing systems of social support, Clinton, like Harper Lee, promoted the idea that welfare creates dependency and corruption in the poor. Like Lee, he promoted the idea of the deserving poor and the undeserving poor. When Bill Clinton transformed welfare into TANF, or Temporary Assistance for Needy Families, his policy makers turned poor children into the "good" deserving poor and their parents into lazy shirkers who deserved punishment and austerity.[11] Neoliberal policies argue that social safety nets do not catch people falling down; they trap people from rising up. For Lee's novelistic support of such views of the poor, she received a Pulitzer Prize, a National Medal of Freedom (from President George W. Bush), and a National Medal of Arts (from President Barack Obama).

The novel predicted the triumphs of the post-1968 PMC: the moral rectitude of the virtuous lawyer and his high-spirited daughter renders the solution to racism attractive to the establishment—work on individual capacities for empathy and walking in another human being's shoes; read books; have righteous feelings. *To Kill a Mockingbird* was an extraordinarily effective piece of Cold War anti-Communist propaganda: based on a liberal fantasy that antiracism is about good white people defending helpless black people against bad (poor) white people, it created an image of American liberalism that was a powerful tool for winning hearts and minds at home and around the world.

11. See Richard Fording and Sanford Schram, "The Welfare Reform Disaster," Jacobin, August 28, 2016, https://prospect.org /features/low-wages-add/.

In July 2015, HarperCollins published *Go Set a Watchman,* a sequel to *To Kill a Mockingbird.* Reviewers were disappointed with *Watchman,* not only in the quality of its writing but also because it revealed that Atticus was a member of the Ku Klux Klan. In the novel, he confesses his affiliation to the grown-up Scout, who now lives in New York City and is home in Alabama on vacation. Although the *New York Times* and Kakutani worried about the bitter disappointment that Lee's fans would experience after discovering that Atticus Finch was a racist, the second novel is proof that Lee was actually an ambivalent propagandist.[12] Historical accounts and archival evidence have long confirmed that Klan membership and lynch mobs were made up of educated, wealthy white people who were upstanding citizens of their communities. Many of them, like Atticus, were educated professionals.[13]

If Lee was trying to correct the false, elitist image of racism promoted by *To Kill a Mockingbird,* Kakutani is oblivious to the writer's attempt at historical self-correction. In fact, Kakutani's 2016 portrait of Obama the reader and the thoughtful man is pure ideology. Obama's bookish empathy had distinct limitations. He deported more undocumented immigrants than any other president before him. The post-2008 bank bailout saved bankers but threw millions of Americans out of their homes as they defaulted on usurious mortgages. Obama governed for Wall Street interests, his hand guided by PMC elites, and not for the working classes and those who were victims of banking chicanery and malfeasance. Was it possible that Obama empathized more with Jamie Dimon, CEO of JP Morgan Chase, than with

12. July 2015, Kakutani reviews *Go Set a Watchman.*

13. Linda Gordon, "Broadside for the Trump Era: The Ku Klux Klan of the 1920s," March 14, 2018, https://www.versobooks.com/blogs/3688-broadside-for-the-trump-era-the-ku-klux-klan-of-the-1920s.

ordinary African American families who lost their homes and livelihoods because of the financial crisis?

In a country that imagined itself uniquely capable of leveling all playing fields and creating equality of opportunity for an astounding array of people of all genders, races, sexualities, gender identifications, and so on, American institutions are increasingly adept at distributing rewards for intelligence and hard work to the few—the suffering and exclusion of the many be damned. In fact, since the 1970s, PMC elites have come to enjoy astounding levels of economic and psychic stability, something to which working-class, non-college-educated people can lay only the feeblest of claims. Furthermore, as Ann Case and Angus Deaton show, a dramatic decline in life expectancy and well-being among middle-aged, non-Hispanic working-class whites without high school degrees has taken on the characteristics of a massive public health epidemic.[14] Unfortunately, *deaths of despair* is a term with which we have all become much too familiar. Unsurprisingly, COVID-19 has proved itself much more lethal in working-class communities of color: PMC workers who can stay home to do their work can enjoy an added health advantage in the age of the pandemic.

At the beginning of the eighteenth century, when the labor of others allowed for European bourgeois elites to use their leisure time to cultivate sensibility and sensitivity in an allegedly disinterested manner, a select group of men and women of leisure came to imagine new forms of sociability and intersubjectivity. Today's capitalists and PMC elites are also into self-cultivation, but their anxiety about their "privilege" makes them work very hard to humiliate others and project themselves tirelessly as a cultural and political vanguard, doing things to themselves of

14. Ann Case and Angus Deaton, *Deaths of Despair and the Future of Capitalism* (Princeton, N.J.: Princeton University Press, 2020).

which ordinary people are incapable. PMC elites are always experimenting with themselves: from returning to the "land" under the aegis of new communalism to keto diets, only drinking sewage-laden raw water, and intermittent fasting, their self-indulgence is always a kind of sanctimonious austerity. In terms of etiquette and new forms of mutual address, PMC elites have pioneered a language of liberal tolerance that the working classes have not mastered. PMC elites, consciously or unconsciously, want to humiliate their adversaries by attributing to them a desperate lack of intelligence, empathy, and virtue.

When Kakutani interviewed Obama and he paraphrased Atticus Finch on how not to be a racist, the PMC elite was deifying a mode of reading that was meant to build a set of weak but socially legible links between people in closed-off, insular worlds of sensibilities and sensitivities. Obama, Kakutani, and the early Harper Lee play important roles in inculcating us with the values of American pluralism, here seen as a top-down lesson in the incorporation of professionalized, liberal protocols of self-improvement. Other people, other experiences, only exist to the extent that they can expand our capacity for empathy and feeling. Obama and Kakutani were teaching us all a lesson about how to deal with our cultural inheritance: their PMC didacticism offers lessons we should refuse to learn. Let us read Atticus Finch as a political project and the novel in which he exists as a piece of well-crafted, anti–welfare state, antisocialist propaganda. Reading matters deeply, but not in the way Obama and Kakutani want it to.

The PMC Has Sex

DURING THE SUMMER OF LOVE, vanguardist May 1968ers thought that they invented new and revolutionary ways of experiencing sexual pleasure. They did not. They thought they were the first sexual adventurers in the course of human history. They were not. Sex has always been a messy affair, but during the eighteenth century in Europe, especially but not exclusively in France, the mostly male libertines who took sexual freedom seriously were writing about scientific inquiry into the observable world, the death of God, the worthiness of non-European cultures, and desecrating the sacraments while they flouted Christian morality by living in differing degrees of sin. They were part of a sexual revolution, and they were very conscious of its political consequences.

In the eighteenth century, French libertine literature was filled with anthropomorphized clitorises, detailed accounts of foot fetishes, and deep discussions of the pleasures of anal penetration. The sexual revolutionary to whom we owe many of our progressive ideals about sex is the Marquis de Sade. An aristocratic class traitor and a hopeless sexual deviant, he was a supporter of the French Revolution who spent much of his life in miserable prison cells writing pornography. Adorno and Horkheimer noted that the modern, European demystification of sexual behavior began with Sade's reasoning about human sexuality and its probing, restless search for pleasure. In a remarkable pamphlet, contained in his pornographic novel of ideas *Philosophy in the Boudoir,* he writes, "Frenchmen, try harder if you want to be republicans." Sade argued that the 1789 revolution may have overturned church and monarchy but that it should go farther if it wanted to free the people and seal its abolition of superstition and oppression. Sexual knowledge—that is, knowledge of how to obtain pleasure with one's body and the bodies of others—should be available to all without prejudice. Libertinage, the exercise of absolute sexual freedom on the part of avowed atheists, had been the exclusive purview of aristocrats under the *ancien régime.* Sade wanted sexual freedom for all, and he warned that if the revolutionaries did not overturn the idols of sexual morality and demand sexual freedom for the people, the powers of church and king would lie in wait, ready to overturn the revolutionary achievements of Danton and Robespierre and the French masses who had finally overthrown both king and church. In short, Sade warned of a counterrevolution if the sexual revolution did not take the logic of emancipation to its limit.

In *Philosophy in the Boudoir,* a bright, fifteen-year-old virgin named Eugenie is initiated into the mysteries of erotic pleasure with men and women by an experienced twenty-six-year-old libertine, Madame de Saint-Ange, who teaches her how to "maximize" her pleasure in sex: in the pamphlet within the novel, Sade argues that adultery, sodomy, prostitution, incest, and rape should all be decriminalized. He turned out to be partially prescient. In 2020 in the United States, sex before and outside of marriage is no longer taboo: outside of extreme religious sects, mothers and fathers do not weep about deflowered sons or sexually experienced daughters. Furthermore, homosexuality has been decriminalized in almost every industrialized democracy in the world, while gay marriage has been legalized in many of these countries as well. The normalization or at least decriminalization of prostitution is seen in liberal democracies as a boon for sex workers and a final step in a liberal, sexually enlightened society. It is hard to deny that Sade was a political visionary—in part. Not all of the taboos Sade listed as oppressive have been lifted by enlightened societies. The dark aspect of his sexual enlightenment, the systematic misuse and abuse of others for one's own pleasure, or sadism, for example, has not become socially acceptable in any situation. Sadism was for Theodor Adorno and Max Horkheimer at the end of World War II a philosophical system that justified the radical coldness of the Enlightenment as the rampant instrumentalization and exploitation and abuse of others—workers, chattel, serfs, and slaves. Adorno and Horkheimer argued that eighteenth-century sentimentality was the obverse of sadism. Both value systems were necessary for the expansion of capitalism: do-goodism and good intentions masking a world conquering reduction of life to profit margins.

The sexual revolutionaries of the 1960s replicated in part the Sadean enlightenment, without acknowledging their Western predecessor: they preferred citing Eastern sexual arts in their innovations. The New Left sexual revolutionaries believed that they had forged a new relationship to pleasure that they wanted to share with the world. Just as they rejected the paltry satisfactions and mass-manufactured goods and TV dinners provided by the affluent society, they rejected old-fashioned ways of having intercourse. From the muddy fields of Woodstock to the fragrant groves of Ken Kesey's compound, the counterculture and the New Left proudly experimented with allegedly novel forms of hedonism that most of the time turned into polygamy for one charismatic male and submission of a group of wan women to his will.

Feminists, unhappy with the primal horde antics of New Left men, discovered that women had to take back their own bodies and, in so doing, their relationship to pleasure. When the Boston Women's Health Book Collective published *Our Bodies, Our Selves,* a female-oriented guide to women's health, they promoted the idea that the establishment had been keeping information about female anatomy and female experience from women. They believed that a compilation of critical information shared in networks of women would lead finally to the full emancipation of female sexuality. If the Sadean heroine was liberated by orgasms, PMC feminists believed instead that it was information about achieving orgasms that was truly emancipatory. College-educated New Left women really thought they were at the vanguard of sex and social life. *Our Bodies* suggested that everything a woman did—learning to repair her car, taking a long hike, going kayaking—was a personal leisure activity that contained incredible political significance. *Our Bodies* insisted that women need to understand their bodies because men deny them access to this magical, frightening, unruly thing. The authors were addressing PMC women when they complained about visiting condescending ob-gyns who were visibly impatient to run off to their tennis matches after quick looks down the speculum. The authors overlooked the fact that most women in the world did not receive regular medical care at all. In a further twist on their "privilege," the authors of *Our Bodies* earnestly told women to explore the pleasures of physical labor, ignoring the fact that the majority of women in the world performed physical labor not out of choice but out of necessity. Throughout human history, women have broken their backs carrying water and farming, while nursing their babies, harvesting fields by hand, washing clothes in rivers, and so on. When women lived in homes without electricity or running water, they did the kinds of work necessary to survive in agricultural economies of the sort that college-educated urban and suburban women could not imagine—except as exotic places to visit in their gap years.

The Industrial Revolution only created more kinds of work for working-class women, some of it physical, some of it based on fine motor skills, but all of it routinized and punishing in its rhythms of production.

In reaction to the hyperbolic ambitions of the women's movement, conservative culture warriors of the 1970s and 1980s promoted a moral panic about the impending dissolution of marriage and the family. But as time passed, countercultural PMC men and women did not become sexual libertines. In fact, the majority of college-educated Americans abandoned promiscuity and nontraditional romantic arrangements as they became more successful in their professions. They were incentivized to settle down and stop cycling through partners as their incomes and assets increased. The protection of PMC socioeconomic status created opportunities for sacrifice and compromise that precarious working-class people abjured. In 2020, it is among non-college-educated people that we find growing rates of divorce and single parenthood. It is truly an ironic reversal in values, upending the logic of the culture wars when PMC families, whether straight or gay, embrace monogamy and family values with greater zeal than their working-class counterparts.

For PMC feminism, the revolution in sex was mostly a revolution in information and education. It was a revolution that could be made by reading a book, or in a consciousness-raising group about reading that book. It was a revolution that made orgasm and pleasure objects of PMC moral and pedagogical refinement (remember the G spot?). To be part of this revolution, you had to accept that the private experiences and lives of elite PMC people were the most important sites of meaningful political and cultural activity. In sex-positive PMC feminism, the best sex could be had in a social vacuum: it would take place in a comfortable bed with clean sheets, between consenting partners free of economic or social anxiety. In such an optimal situation, a woman could finger her clitoris, labia, or perineum in a leisurely manner, all the while communicating her needs and desires to a sensitive and receptive partner. Good sex became suffused with the logic of information and communication theory upon which ideals of consent are built.

In stark contrast to sexually enlightened PMC people, working-class men and women were represented in popular culture of the 1970s as trapped in misogyny, homophobia, prejudice, and violence, out of touch with their feelings and unable to communicate their erotic needs.[1] For New Left creatives and liberals working in Hollywood in the 1970s, working-class people were living in the sexual dark ages. Working-class men were hopelessly authoritarian and working-class women unwittingly submissive to the patriarchal power of a family wage earner. Whereas at the turn of the nineteenth century, the working class had been undeniably at the vanguard of political struggles against capitalists and their proxies, the PMC after 1968 asserted that it alone was at the vanguard of all revolutions, including and above all the sexual revolution.

Under the Obama administration, the state became intensely involved in the enlightened regulation of sex. From 2008, PMC triumphalism under the well-spoken and well-read president channeled the collective energy of liberals to focus on sex in one of the most important sites of class formation: university campuses, especially elite university campuses. Instrumentalized obsession with sexual violence and sexual excess is an important part of American Puritanism: moral and virtuous superiority in the sexual enlightenment makes up an important part of the countercultural inheritance of the PMC. Rather than focusing on economic malfeasance, an ascendant PMC elite under Obama

---

1. Jefferson Cowie, *Stayin' Alive: The Last Days of the Working Class* (New York: New Press, 2012).

pursued sexual crimes—not at work or in the workplace but on college campuses—with a zeal that liberals reserve for any policy that diverts attention away from economic redistribution. In short, rather than break up the banks or reform the financial sector after he took office, Obama wanted to use his electoral victory to eliminate sexual violence on college campuses. In 2011, his Department of Education Office for Civil Rights sent a "Dear Colleague" letter to more than seven thousand universities warning them that if they did not take action to prevent and remedy sexual violence and sexual assault on their campuses, they would risk losing their rights to all federal funding. Legal commentators today admit that college administrations reacted to the letter with overcompliance. Many Title IX offices rejected innocent-until-proven-guilty principles that form the democratic rule of law and set up campus investigative panels and bodies that became little more than kangaroo courts.[2]

At the same time, sensational stories of sexual violence and sexual abuse on college campuses emerged in the mainstream media, as if to confirm the necessity of the Obama administration's stringent new policies. In 2015, at the height of the Obama-era sex panic, Kirby Dick's *The Hunting Ground* was released by—wait for it—the Weinstein Company. Dick's documentary presented college campuses as terrifying places for young women to live. Dick, with the help of Harvey Weinstein, pandered to his liberal audience's thirst for stories about campus sexual violence. In 2016, Amber Frost cited the National Crime Victimization Survey numbers showing that non-college-going women were 1.2 times more likely to be sexually assaulted than their college-going counterparts.[3] Sexual vio-

2. https://www.newyorker.com/news/our-columnists/assessing -betsy-devos-proposed-rules-on-title-ix-and-sexual-assault.
3. Amber Frost, "The Trouble with the Trauma Industry," *Baffler*, no. 31 (June 2016), https://thebaffler.com/salvos/confession-booth-frost.

lence on college campuses attracted liberal PMC elites to a new front in the culture wars, far away from inequality, oppression, and workplace sexual harassment and discrimination. Fighting sexual violence on campus allowed the PMC to reinforce its belief that white-collar professionals and lawyers like Atticus Finch were the true heroes in low-risk struggles against anything but economic abuse.

Rolling Stone, a magazine born in the crucible of the rock 'n' roll, drug-fueled, libertine counterculture of San Francisco in 1967, covered one of the most lurid campus sexual violence stories of the Obama era. The magazine was once a highly successful media outlet for the rock 'n' roll–fueled generation of middle-class consumers with growing buying power. By 2014, it had become just another mainstream magazine competing for eyeballs on the internet. The economic crisis of 2008 hit the magazine particularly hard. Ad revenues for print magazines peaked in 2007 and declined steadily year after year, with no respite from either digital sales or the supposed economic "recovery" engineered by the Bush and Obama administrations.[4] It is quite understandable that when contributing editor Sabrina Erdely uncovered the story of an alleged gang rape at the University of Virginia (UVA), Jan Wenner and *Rolling Stone*'s editorial board rushed to publish her piece, "Rape on Campus." The nine-thousand-word story detailed from the point of view of "Jackie," the alleged victim, a horrifying gang rape that had taken place at the Phi Beta Kappa Psi fraternity house in 2012. The story got 2.7 million online views on *Rolling Stone*'s site, more than any other noncelebrity feature the magazine had ever published. When the *Washington*

4. Kali Hays, "Magazine Ad Revenue Continues to Decline Despite Some Audience Growth," *WWD,* July 27, 2019, https://wwd .com/business-news/media/magazines-ad-revenue-continues-decline -despite-some-audience-growth-1203224173/.

Post decided to launch an independent investigation into Jackie's story, it became apparent that Erdely had not corroborated any of the details that Jackie had given her. Among the many gaps in Jackie's story, the *Washington Post* reporters discovered that there was no record of a party at the frat house on the night Jackie alleged she was raped. In 2015, the magazine published a retraction of the story along with a detailed forensic investigation into Erdely's journalistic failings performed by a team from the Columbia School of Journalism.[5] *Rolling Stone* and Sabrina Erdely were then sued by the fraternity Phi Beta Kappa Psi and by Nicole Eramo, dean of students at UVA, for defamation. The wider, cultural and political consequences of such a flagrant case of professional failure are difficult to assess, but the Right certainly knew how to inflame popular hatred and resentment of the "mainstream media" and professional journalists and it took full advantage of this flagrant failure in reporting. Far right news site *The Daily Caller* became obsessed with the case and gloated over *Rolling Stone*'s and Erdely's disgrace and legal troubles. For the Conservatives and the far right incubators of incel anger, the UVA story confirmed their narrative: liberal media were filled with sensation-seeking hypocrites looking to cash in on fake news stories demonizing young men.[6]

Fifty years after the Summer of Love, college-going women were armed with more information and more sex educa-

5. Sheila Coronel, Steve Coll, and Derek Kravitz, "Rolling Stone and UVA: The Columbia University Graduate School Report: An Anatomy of Journalistic Failure," https://www.rollingstone.com/culture/culture-news/rolling-stone-and-uva-the-columbia-university-graduate-school-of-journalism-report-44930/.

6. Lucia Graves, "Five Years On, the Lessons from the Rolling Stone Rape Story," *Guardian,* December 29, 2019, https://www.theguardian.com/society/2019/dec/29/rolling-stone-rape-story-uva-five-years.

tion than any generation before them, but they seemed less capable of assuming sexual agency and more in need of protection than previous generations of women, who had had to deal with sexual autonomy and male desire without the help of university Title IX officers. For Laura Kipnis, self-described "left-wing feminist," "rebel," and freethinker and professor at Northwestern University, we were living through a new period of sexual paranoia. Kipnis's account of her own Title IX investigation and the case against her former Northwestern colleague Peter Ludlow, make up the heart of her book on this topic, *Unwanted Advances: Sexual Paranoia Comes to Campus.*[7] Kipnis presents a clear, evenhanded account of the Kafkaesque Title IX investigation launched against her after she published a series of articles about Northwestern and Peter Ludlow's case in the *Chronicle of Higher Education.*[8] The first half of Kipnis's book is about the accusations against the philosophy professor and the Title IX investigation that Northwestern launched against both Ludlow and Kipnis herself. Kipnis concludes that section with the observation that even though Ludlow was certainly guilty of inappropriate behavior with an undergraduate and a graduate student, the loss of his job as punishment was entirely incommensurate with his crime, which Kipnis describes as motivated by naive childishness rather than raw abuse and exploitation. In the second half of *Unwanted Advances,* Kipnis summarizes many of the stories of the abuse of Title IX that she heard after going public as the subject of a Title IX investiga-

7. Laura Kipnis, *Unwanted Advances: Sexual Paranoia Comes to Campus* (New York: HarperCollins, 2017).

8. Laura Kipnis, "Sexual Paranoia Strikes Academe," *Chronicle of Higher Education,* February 27, 2015, https://www.chronicle.com/article/Sexual-Paranoia-Strikes/190351, and Kipnis, "My Title IX Inquisition," *Chronicle of Higher Education,* May 29, 2015.

tion herself. For her trouble, Kipnis became a target of campus feminists and activists, but Kipnis would not be silenced. She is a liberal, a high liberal, which is the very best kind of liberal there is. She believes in robust debate and vigorous public dissent in the university, and her presentation of the abuse of Title IX is a courageous act in the cancel culture demonization of anyone who dares to question the protocols and assumptions behind sexual harassment investigations on college campuses.

For Kipnis, the worst thing about sexual paranoia is that it makes us "dumb." Sex panics provide "a formula for intellectual rigidity." She blames the witch hunt atmosphere on campuses for undermining the traditional ideals of the university—as a refuge for freethinkers, who are now being buried by an "avalanche of platitudes and fear."[9] The ideal university that Kipnis cherishes is a fantasy built on the social ideal of an egalitarian society, where students and professors are libertine-like freethinkers, free of material want. While this ideal was operative between 1945 and 1972, intensifying inequality and the increasing cost of higher education have destroyed this mid-century American idea of the university. In Kipnis's fantasy university, everyone lives in the affluent society: therein lies the basis of her ideal of intellectual freedom. Kipnis came of age at the tail end of an unprecedented expansion of higher education in the United States, and she exudes the confidence and bravado of someone who has not known real professional or economic insecurity. She is remarkably cut off from the torture chamber buzz of anxiety that afflicts students today. She gives sexual paranoia too much credit for the intellectual torpor of contemporary university life: in my experience, professional and economic insecurity is the greatest thought inhibitor of all.

9. Kipnis, *Unwanted Advances.*

In concluding *Unwanted Advances*, Kipnis presents a cogent analysis of an epidemic of college blackout drinking while presenting the moral panic of our times as related to the incomplete emancipation of female sexuality. She believes that the problems of campus sex can be solved with more education for men and women on the topic of sexual ambivalence, consent, and agency. What if overvaluation of information and "education" is actually part of the problem with coming of age under neoliberalism and its austerity policies? What if competition for places at institutions of higher education and the higher and higher barrier of entry to the PMC are actually what fuels the sex panics that make us all more stupid? In a society that sees education as a private good, an asset to be used to compete in an increasingly precarious and uncertain world, most young people do not feel as if they can afford to be curious or pleasure seeking while in college. The intellectual and erotic freedoms cherished by Kipnis are shaped by a kind of aristocratic libertine thought enabled by mid-century American principles of economic redistribution and equality that contemporary university administrations neither understand nor support.

The Obama administration's zealous enforcement of Title IX is very different from the way in which Hank Paulson and Timothy Geithner engineered the bailout of criminal financial institutions after the financial meltdown of 2008. Why didn't the Obama administration send a "Dear Colleague" letter to investment bankers and financial advisors, warning them about helping their clients evade billions of dollars in taxes, taxes that used correctly could be reinvested in public universities and public education programs? What about a "Dear Colleague" letter addressed to Big Pharma, warning it about federal regulations coming down the pipeline about opioid dumping in rural areas? What about a "Dear Colleague" letter addressed to Wells Fargo, Goldman Sachs, AIG, JP Morgan Chase, Bank of America, or

any other institution that insured, sold, and packaged bad mortgages to the detriment of borrowers and investors? What about
"Dear Colleague" letters to fossil fuel companies warning them
about their cover-up about their knowledge of carbon production and climate change? In the absence of such letters, we have
to conclude that PMC elites prefer fomenting moral panics to
implementing even the most modest redistributive or progressive economic policies, even after a global financial catastrophe.

To close out our discussion of campus sex panics, we have to
turn to the story of Emma Sulkowicz. In 2015, Sulkowicz gradu-
ated from Columbia University with a BA in visual arts, for which
her performance *Mattress Performance: Carry That Weight* ful-
filled a degree requirement. Sulkowicz's piece was staged as a
protest and "performance" against the fact that her 2013 allega-
tions of rape against fellow undergraduate Paul Nungesser had
not led to any consequences for him and that he was allowed to
continue being a student at Columbia. Sulkowicz had wanted
him expelled for the alleged attack, but after an internal inquiry,
Columbia University found Nungesser without responsibility for
the alleged assault. Sulkowicz was furious about the findings, and
she spent her senior year on the campus carrying the mattress
upon which the alleged violation took place. Sulkowicz's sense of
revanchist entitlement, her confident disregard for due process
(the centerpiece of liberalism's rule of law), her indifference to
privacy—of her alleged attacker and her own—became realized
in her "performance" as art.

Like all endurance-based performance art, the senseless ex-
penditure of physical effort is a display of the elites' absolute
freedom from the necessity of physical labor. From this point
of view, Sulkowicz's performance of mattress carrying makes a
mockery of the physicality of manual labor. Most workers in the
world still labor with their bodies and have to endure physical
pain and hardship during a day's work: to "choose" physical

endurance is the ultimate sign of PMC sovereignty. It should go without saying that Sulkowicz first and foremost objectified her own trauma. The performance allowed her a degree of dissociation, but it also gave her the platform upon which to make a bid for visibility, notoriety, fame, and celebrity. She became a one-woman placard, publicizing a traumatic experience to make public something she had to endure in private. Sulkowicz as an artist, and a child of PMC elites (her parents are successful business psychologists in Manhattan), was responding to, commenting on, and reproducing the regime of postindustrial work, a kind of work that entails the constant production of publicity-garnering activity in the name of self-branding. In the pursuit of justice, Sulkowicz became famous for her ability to turn private pain into public spectacle.

One of the most notorious artists of the internet age, Ryan Trecartin also works on new media celebrity by staging performances of crazy parties gone wrong and gone wild. His video performances are carnivalesque, nonsensical, drug-addled events characterized by generalized dissolution, abjection, and thwarted pleasure seeking. Trecartin advertises himself as self-taught, campy, messy, and working class. Sulkowicz's art partook of the craving for fame that animates all of Trecartin's work, but she had a different aim in advertising her traumatic sexual experiences: her art was made out of her frustration about Nungesser's impunity. After graduating from Columbia, Sulkowicz was admitted into the highly selective Whitney Program, a year-long residency for art stars in the making, and her follow-up artistic work continued on the register of sexual sensationalism and art world prestige economy anxiety: she began with *Ceci n'est pas un viol* (This is not a rape), a video restaging of her rape. She also had herself tied up by an S&M professional she called "Mr. Whitney" while she wore a white bikini emblazoned with a *W* and an *M*, standing for, we assume, "Whitney Museum." Her inane personal statements about her work parrot the tired truisms about female empowerment and the need to counter criticism of "fem bodies."

Hailed by both performance artist Marina Abramovic and *New York Times* art critic Roberta Smith as a genius, Sulkowicz proved ambivalent about her art world success. In 2017, she did a performance piece as a therapist at the fake Healing Touch Integral Wellness Center in Philadelphia. *Bustle* magazine praised her new work for resisting Trump.[10] But then, two years later, in 2019, she was featured in the *Cut* hanging around alt-light, men's rights types who were once her biggest haters online. Sulkowicz claimed that she had become open to their point of view. She also claimed to be tired of contemporary art and said that she was quitting being an artist.[11] In the meantime, her alleged attacker, Paul Nungesser, and Columbia University settled out of court a lawsuit in which Nungesser successfully sued the university for gender discrimination based on Title IX. For liberals, sexual violence on campus is of critical importance because (1) universities are sites of class reproduction, and all intersubjective encounters in such places must be rationalized, and (2) the PMC elite loves to play the virtuous hero in clear-cut moral dramas where economic exploitation is not an issue. Laura Kipnis should not have been surprised by the fact that a segment of PMC young people no longer sees sex as an activity where pleasure and agency are critical. For Emma Sulkowicz, everything that happens to her can be instrumentalized and turned into fodder for publicity and prosecution. The lack of boundaries between the personal and

10. Gabrielle Moss, "Emma Sulkowicz's Plan to Resist Trump," *Bustle,* February 7, 2017, https://www.bustle.com/p/heres-how-emma -sulkowicz-the-columbia-mattress-artist-plans-to-resist-trump-34456.

11. Sylvie McNamara, "Did Emma Sulkowicz Get Redpilled?," *Cut,* October 28, 2019, https://www.thecut.com/2019/10/did-emma -sulkowicz-mattress-performance-get-redpilled.html.

the political is the poisoned fruit of contemporary neoliberalism's metabolization of the historical counterculture.

If the case of Harvey Weinstein lies outside of the purview of my critique of sex panics, it is because Jodi Kantor and Megan Twohey focused on workplace sexual assault, corroborated by countless victims and employees of the former movie mogul.[12] It would be wonderful if we could extend the investigative attention and care paid to Harvey Weinstein's victims to other workers who have been exploited and abused in far less glamorous workplaces. In Kantor and Twohey's reporting, Weinstein's victims were terrified of him because of the power he wielded over their careers and professional prospects. It is clear that sexual coercion and economic insecurity work together to create conditions for abuse. There is no sexual freedom or pleasure without freedom from the terrifying economic fear for simple survival to which so many of us are reduced. Weinstein's Sadean treatment of women would not have been possible without the professional and economic power that he wielded over an entire industry. Kipnis, like Sade, believes in a world of sexual adventure without economic coercion—that world is certainly desirable but not realizable under the current conditions wrought by capitalism and its narrowing spaces of authentic intersubjective experience.

12. Jodi Kantor and Megan Twohey, *She Said: Breaking the Sexual Harassment Story That Launched a Movement* (New York: Penguin, 2019).

Conclusion

MARX'S *CAPITAL* WAS A WORLD teeming with raw materials and active agents fighting and working with each other, engaged in the processes of production to wrest wealth from raw materials like gold, iron, wool, and cotton: for Marx, these workers would make history when they revolted against capitalism. PMC elite workers also see themselves as the makers of history. They labor in a world of floating signifiers, statistics, analytics, projections, predictions and identity performativity, virtue signaling, and affectual production. Their loves and lives are both virtual and disembodied. Their work continues unabated despite the ravages of the COVID-19 pandemic. People trained in this regime of symbolic manipulation love to weaponize outrage to fuel moral panics, but they are unable and unwilling to face their identity as a class. In the liberal professions, they police each other to enforce the sort of social and intellectual conformity required by their class, one that is fundamentally fragmented by competition and individualism. All PMC-approved policies about inequality, racism, and bias circle back to strengthening their sense of political agency and cultural and moral superiority. In a viciously competitive market environment, they have abandoned once cherished professional standards of research while fetishizing transgression, or better yet, the performance of transgression.

Despite its veneer of detached sophistication, the PMC embraces melodrama and sentimentality when dealing with inequality, imagining powerless people as innocent victims who it alone is uniquely able to "help." The PMC desperately wants to be a gender-neutral Atticus Finch. For Marx, the unique industrial processes of labor formed the vanguard class of industrial capitalism. Managers and professionals were unfortunately never part of that class, but their complicity with capital is something they want to disguise as "resilience" and "flexibility," qualities that working-class losers do not possess in the PMC worldview. Workers remade the industrial world, but today's PMC elites resent the revolutionary power of the leftism of the past. They want to manage social change and a possible revolution even as their own functions are constrained by the ideological demands of the ruling class. Even though they understand the futility of their own work, they do not believe in the systemic changes necessary to remake economic systems that would allow the many to find rewarding work and lead meaningful lives of dignity and economic security.

In historicizing the PMC's ideological investments, I am not simply trying to "understand" its identity to add to a precious repository of scholastic knowledge. I am interested in criticizing its values in order to abandon its politics. To build a socialist future, we have to engage in a constant struggle to overcome the political paralysis to which both centrism and pseudo-radicalism lead. Across the world, ordinary people without college degrees have rejected PMC technocracy in favor of populist authoritarianism because they no longer believe in the dominant neoliberal narrative about austerity and competition. To the majority of non-college-educated people, the PMC increasingly appear as pedantic, hypocritical, and punishing: in authoritarian, science denying conservative leaders, they recognize their own helpless rage and ignorance. In angry demagogues, they find the embodiment of a sovereignty they have been denied. Of course, their support for billionaire populists and their minions is entirely reactionary, but the political answer to populism is not liberal reformism or moderate centrism. It is committed socialism. If the PMC still insists that a little bit of economic redistribution should be managed carefully by corporate friendly "experts," socialists have to demand a different order of politics and a different calculation of political engagement, one which aims at building solidarity in the shadow of a distant revolutionary horizon.

Dear reader, you are probably like me, a member of the PMC, or at least you have been educated in its institutions. I hope that this short introduction to the false consciousness of a class that still wants to believe itself a heroic and virtuous political actor will strengthen the reader's resolve to reject PMC politics while building on this critique of its reactionary class positions. Having been imbued with its ethos and its ideology, we all have to work to undo the effects of PMC propaganda to join the class war from below. This brief introduction serves as a guide to identifying PMC values in ourselves, the better to liquidate them. Because of the ideological distortions of leftist politics by PMC values, self-criticism must be the beginning of all political engagement. We have to abandon the way the PMC wants us to think about success, intelligence, racism, violence, children, reading, health care, well-being, pleasure, and sex. We have to reject making a virtue out of taste and consumption habits. We have to understand ourselves as the universal subject of a history dominated by capitalism's dynamic, exploitative, and punishing powers. It will not be easy, because PMC elites control so much of our lives and quietly threaten us with exclusion if we do not follow their sanctioned lines of milquetoast politics.

The PMC would have us forget that as a class, it has served capitalism and the profit motive very well: tragically, it has also been hugely successful at monopolizing the language of progressive and enlightened politics, even as it has abandoned the best aspects of liberal professionalism and the democratic culture in which such ideas of intellectual autonomy can thrive. The values of professionalism, with its disinterested call for accountability and respect of truths arrived at by a community of researchers, are critical to building socialism. Professionalism is not the enemy of solidarity. Professionalism and its disciplinary limits are necessary for nurturing socialist specialists who will be needed to oversee massive economic redistribution and the strengthening of public infrastructure and public goods that will be necessary for the environmental survival of the planet and the political survival of democracy.

I am finishing this manuscript in the middle of the coronavirus pandemic lockdown. The economic and public health disaster that we are experiencing in the United States is directly linked to the power of for-profit health care interests and corporations in hollowing out public services and public health. The fact that the Biden–Harris administration is opposed to national health care, or Medicare for All, is very revealing. Rather than promoting national health care, a phalanx of centrist experts will promote individual actions, such as mask wearing, as the new "virtues." Yes, we should wear masks, but we should demand free COVID-19 testing and contact tracing, free vaccines along with the rebuilding of public health institutions to serve public health and not the profit motive. If times go back to normal, and your boss or health insurer tries to sell you on the commodification of your health as a "wellness" protocol, remember that health care is part of public infrastructure, not a commodity. Just as provision for quality childcare for every family should be part of public infrastructure, so should the care of the elderly and the sick be priority areas of public investment. My goal is simple: help normalize socialist economics and politics in the face of the concerted demonization of its vision of what is collectively possible. Socialism itself is neither glamorous nor innovative: it does not sprinkle its agendas with new pronouns or fancy neologisms. Its signifiers do not float on air or ether: its policies should be tethered to good statistics, objective reality, and the power and uncertainty of scientific method and reason. A socialist intellectual should refuse to wear the cloaks of virtue, erudition, and detachment: she should be prepared to enter the field of class struggle on the side of workers and the exploited. Conservative and progressive PMC elites and the institutions they control are actively hostile to worker power and socialism as such. Therefore solidarity and organization are more critical than ever to long-term political struggle. Affect-driven protests, raucous crowds, and violent rioting may provide the political openings for social change, but political transformation at the scale we need demands discipline of the kind the academic Left is used to condemning. While a mixed economy may be the short-term reality that we dare hope for, let's strengthen the hand of the socialist aspects of that hybrid system. While the PMC promotes the hoarding of capital and virtue, we must detach ourselves from its crypto-Puritanical regulation of human appetites and human relations. We must be heretics. We should blaspheme.

The PMC elite has refused to name the economic system that has ruined our planet, undermined our trust in public institutions, destroyed public health, diminished our childhoods, and litigated our pleasures. Neither evil nor virtuous, the PMC is a secular and material antagonist. In calling out capitalism as the enemy of the people, we must also name our enemy's most assiduous courtier and sycophant: the professional managerial class.

Acknowledgments

I THANK LEO AND PETER KRAPP for putting up with my rants about the meritocracy. They helped me have courage. Thank you, Leo, for being such a great coauthor and son. Francois Cusset, Thierry Labica, and Wang Chaohua invited me to Université de Paris Ouest and Tsinghua University, respectively, to give talks that formed the basis of these chapters. Finally, I want to thank Ara Merjian for inviting me to talk about 1968 at NYU in Berlin. For all those conversations, I am very grateful. Thank you, Megan Kilpatrick, for publishing me on the topic of socialism, childhood, and care in Jacobin and helping me think through ideas about psychoanalysis and the collective social well-being. Melissa Naschek helped me with the critical discussions about the 1619 Project. Alex Hochuli, George Hoare, and Phillip Cunliffe were critical in helping me formulate many of the ideas in the book. Thank you, Connor Kilpatrick, for our conversations about sex panics. Tyrus Miller, Thomas Williams, and Kelly Donahey kept me thinking about critical theory in ways that were invigorating. In addition, this book simply would not have been possible without the comradeship of Amber Frost, John-Baptiste Oduor, and Jarek Ervin, who kept me focused during dark times and made me feel part of a bigger collective project. Our book with Doctrinaire Press will be out soon. The encouragement and support I received from Leah Pennywark, Jason Weidemann, Anne Carter, and Douglas Armato at the University of Minnesota Press allowed me to complete a project that I fully expected to be canceled. Finally, I have to acknowledge the neighborhood in which this book was written: University Hills in Irvine and its active Listserv are hot spots of professional managerial class sensibilities and politics. I learned so much from you. In the eternal words of my late Latin teacher at the City of University of New York, "Disco Inferno" or "I learn in Hell." He taught me while he was very ill with complications from AIDS in the early 1990s. I dedicate this book to everyone with whom I shared the dance floor in that other time, in that other pandemic.

(Continued from page iii)

Forerunners: Ideas First

Davide Panagia
Ten Theses for an Aesthetics of Politics

David Golumbia
The Politics of Bitcoin: Software as Right-Wing Extremism

Sohail Daulatzai
Fifty Years of *The Battle of Algiers*: Past as Prologue

Gary Hall
The Uberfication of the University

Mark Jarzombek
Digital Stockholm Syndrome in the Post-Ontological Age

N. Adriana Knouf
How Noise Matters to Finance

Andrew Culp
Dark Deleuze

Akira Mizuta Lippit
Cinema without Reflection: Jacques Derrida's Echopoiesis and Narcissism Adrift

Sharon Sliwinski
Mandela's Dark Years: A Political Theory of Dreaming

Grant Farred
Martin Heidegger Saved My Life

Ian Bogost
The Geek's Chihuahua: Living with Apple

Shannon Mattern
Deep Mapping the Media City

Steven Shaviro
No Speed Limit: Three Essays on Accelerationism

Jussi Parikka
The Anthrobscene

Reinhold Martin
Mediators: Aesthetics, Politics, and the City

John Hartigan Jr.
Aesop's Anthropology: A Multispecies Approach

Catherine Liu is professor of film and media studies at the University of California, Irvine. She is the author of *Copying Machines: Taking Notes for the Automaton* (Minnesota, 2000) and the novel *Oriental Girls Desire Romance* (2012) and is coeditor of *The Dreams of Interpretation: A Century down the Royal Road* (Minnesota, 2007).